The Consecrated Cross-Eyed Bear

The Consecrated Cross-Eyed Bear

Stories from the Less-Solemn Side of Church Life

Charles Allbright

August House Publishers, Inc.

L I T T L E   R O C K

Published by August House, Inc.,
P.O. Box 3223, Little Rock, Arkansas, 72203,
501-372-5450.

Printed in the United States of America
10 9 8 7 6 5 4 3 2

LIBRARY OF CONGRESS CATALOGING-IN-PUBLICATION DATA

Allbright, Charles W.
The consecrated cross-eyed bear : stories from the less-solemn
side of church life / humor by Charles W. Allbright — 1st ed.
p.   cm.
ISBN 0-87483-159-8 (alk. paper) : $8.95
1. Christian life—Humor. 2. Christian life—Anecdotes.
3. Christianity—Arkansas. 4. Arkansas—Religious life and
customs. I. Title.
BV4517.A49   1990
277.67'082'0207—dc20   90-26954

First Edition, 1991

Executive: Ted Parkhurst
Project editor: Judith Faust
Cover design: Bill Jennings
Typography: Lettergraphics, Little Rock

This book is printed on archival-quality paper which meets the
guidelines for performance and durability of the Committee on
Production Guidelines for Book Longevity of the
Council on Library Resources.

AUGUST HOUSE, INC.   PUBLISHERS   LITTLE ROCK

*This book is dedicated to
those who love the Lord.
To those who don't,
a heartfelt "So long!"*

Contents

Signs and Wonders 63

(Re)Called by God 77

Out of the Mouths of Babes 103

In the Presence of the Lord?   *133*

Suffer The Little Children

Suffer The Little Children

Jerome Tilley of Pine Bluff was driving east of Asheville, North Carolina, listening to a radio minister.

The minister was upset about the church's loss of young people.

Outraged was more like it.

"We're not holding our children!"

Jerome Tilley could have heard a pin drop through his radio speaker.

"Where are our children this morning?"

The owner of the voice could not have been far from the pulpit microphone.

"We're right here!" a small worshipper shouted. "And you don't have to holler about it!"

Some churches will do anything to hold their children.

Take the Baptists at Dardanelle.

Take young Sara Knight, daughter of Susan and Jack Knight.

Jack Knight coaches the Dardanelle Sand Lizards football team. His daughter is no ordinary child. She once was tweaked by Paul (Bear) Bryant. Where? At Tuscaloosa, Alabama. Sara Knight was too young to remember that nose tweak. She will not be allowed to forget it.

She will not forget that morning in church, either.

Her dad was an usher, passing the collection plate.

"Jack noticed some kind of commotion in the vicinity of the pew where Susan and Sara were sitting."

A relative describes the Sunday morning service at First Baptist Church at Dardanelle.

The closer Coach Knight drew, the more it looked like the exact pew.

By the time he got there, he was ready to fumble the plate.

"It's her arm," Susan Knight fretted. "Sara's caught in the hymnal rack."

Jack Knight whispered assurances.

"Just take it easy. We'll have it right out of there."

Many faces turned toward the rescue, none more hopefully than Sara Knight's.

She was stuck in there tighter than Chinese handcuffs. The more Jack Knight tried, the worse things got.

"Hell's fire!" a lesser person might have said.

There is nothing Christian about leaving Sara Knight armlocked to the pew.

Her eyes were as big as collection plates, and her mother was shouting whispers to keep calm when Coach Knight bolted from First Baptist.

"Fortunately, they live just a block away. Jack told Sara to stay where she was. He ran home to get a screwdriver, then ran back and unscrewed the songbook rack from the back of the pew. Finally he got her out of there. I doubt that anybody heard much of the sermon."

Suffer the little children.

A Small, Happy Voice

Next to a resounding "Amen!" it was the most gratifying thing the Rev. Thomas Haley could have heard.

Thomas M. Haley is pastor of Dermott United Methodist Church.

At the close of last Sunday's sermon, in that first moment of hush, a small voice rang out, sharp and clear, through the congregation.

"Mommy, that was fun!"

The minister was delighted.

Joining the congregation in laughter, he instructed the youth, "Say it again, son. They didn't hear you."

The fun had been had by John Thomas Haley, three-year-old son of the minister himself.

"As his father, I will remember this day. I will also give him due consideration when the time arrives for him to ask for the car."

Deliver Us From Long, Waspish Sermons

In the bulletin received by members of Pulaski Heights United Methodist Church, the Rev. James B. Argue wrote about the passing of an old year and the coming of a new one.

"There is a sort of feeling that we have an abundance of time coming to us with a whole new year stretching out before us, which isn't true, of course. We have no more time right now than we had last month or six months ago. We just get twenty-four hours a day. We do have control over how we use the time before us. Preachers can preach shorter or longer or about the same as always. Incidentally, the longest sermon on record was delivered by Clinton Locy of West Richland, Washington, in February, 1955. It lasted 48 hours and 18 minutes. Keep that in mind when you complain about the length of my sermons."

Prior to that 48-hour number at West Richland, the longest sermon in histroy was delivered on a July Sunday back in the late 1930s after certain McGehee youngsters were told that if they behaved in chuch that morning as previously, then it would follow as the night the day that all would be at least killed and probably worse.

There was to be not one squirm, one fidget, or one eye-bat, not even if the church caught fire or was swallowed up by an earthquake.

There was no fire that morning, and no earthquake.

But nine yellowjackets had taken up building something on the back of the pew ahead, just inches from the youngsters' bare knees.

When the sermon finally ended, the children had aged about ninety years.

A lady we know says that the last whipping she ever got was because of some sluggish wasps that took up residence in a Reformed Presbyterian Curch in south Pope County.

We assumed she set up a commotion of some sort, trying to escape the wasps.

But that was not it.

"I got it for killing the wasps by smashing them inside a song book."

Communion Confusion

All week long the talk at church was about a big money-raising feast coming Sunday.

But then when a five-year-old boy named Jeffrey went forward and knelt with his mother, all that got served was a cracker crumb and a few drops of grape juice.

Jeffrey could not keep the disgust out of his voice.

Arising, he fumed at his mother, "I thought we were going to have hamburgers!"

Dr. Robert Moore, Jr., of Bauxite reported that incident.

Dr. Moore remembers back when his father was preaching in Camden.

"It was almost time for school to start. Folks were back from their summer vacations."

One family had been all the way out to Las Vegas.

A six-year-old son named Eddie was still full of the trip.

On Communion Sunday, after he and his mother partook and headed back up the aisle, Eddie whispered loud enough for everyone to hear, "Mom! You forgot to pay for our drinks!"

Concerned about the spiritual growth of her two young granddaughters, a North Little Rock woman went by on Sunday morning, gathered the youngsters up, and personally hauled them to church.

The girls are about six and eight.

About some things, the less said, the better. Goodness knows, their mother was brought up properly. Now? She seems to have lost all direction. You'd think she needed tickets to get into church.

Well, these things work themselves out. Or if they don't, then they don't.

But grandmother saw her own duty. On Sunday morning, she went by and gathered up the girls. The three of them went to the church house.

"She learned right away they had to be separated."

This was a neighbor talking. A man to whom the grandmother confided details of her Sunday missionary work.

"The church pew was unfamiliar territory to these young ladies. Right off they started badgering each other, getting into it."

The grandmother rearranged everybody, positioning herself between the girls.

It worked nicely until the communion tray came along.

"You know how very still it gets during a communion service," the neighbor said. "That's how still it was when these young girls reached across their grandmother's lap, clinked their galsses, and said loud enough for everybody in the sanctuary to hear, 'Cheers!'"

It was "World Communion Sunday" at First United Methodist Church of Pocahontas. From his seat up front in the choir, John Malone reflected on the proceedings.

"There were scriptures about communion. Hymns about communion. A sermon about communion by the pastor, Sherman Waters."

Then came the taking of communion itself.

"This lasted about fifteen or twenty minutes. Kathy Blackwell, the organist, played for the length of the communion service, and when the last people were served, she ended with a customary organ closing."

In that brief moment before Mr. Waters could get up and send everybody home, it came from the balcony—a small voice—"Ta-DAAH!"

John Malone was not quick enough.

"In the instant it took me to look up, I saw zilch. Every young person in the balcony was sitting perfectly still, and every parent's hand was moving back toward his or her lap. No smiles, no bruises, nothing."

But down underneath... "Below the balcony, where the older crowd sits, there were lots of smiles, plenty of giggles, and even some tears from over-smiling and over-giggling."

Malone had to report this communion Sunday incident, even without identification.

"If it gets in the newspaper, some Methodist parent will clip it and put it in a scrapbook. But the rest of us will never know who it was."

One Sunday elsewhere, communion almost wasn't. Bob Moore recalls it.

"Dad was in the Hope District. But that particular Sunday, he held a quarterly conference at a little church way back up in the hills near Mena."

Shortly after he arrived, two ladies of the church approached.

"Dr. Moore, we haven't had communion all year. Could we have it today?"

Dr. Moore said of course.

"Get it all set up. We'll have the service right after the sermon."

The ladies disappeared. And a short time later reappeared.

One said, "We can't find any grape juice."

The visiting minister thought a moment.

"See whether you can find a Grapette soda."

Again the ladies went away. And again they returned empty-handed. But with a possibility.

They found a church member who the day before had put up some, well, some persimmon wine.

"But she says it hasn't had time to ferment, or anything."

Dr. Moore said, "Go get it."

In due course, the communion service was held.

After which, according to Robert Moore, Jr., his dad addressed the congregation and directed, "Shall we be standing and whistle the Doxology."

Tithes and Offerings

One minute the collection plate was heading toward her, and the next minute, for some reason, it stopped. This was at Pleasant Valley Church of Christ. Pat Best turned to see what the holdup was.

Next to her in the pew, a woman and a small boy about two years old were struggling for some coins.

The youngster had a death grip on the money, having fished it from the plate. The mother was tugging mightily, squeezing his arm, trying to open the small fist.

At last she succeeded, wrenching the coins free and dropping them back into the plate.

The boy let out a blood-curdling shriek.

The mother grabbed up some coins, stuffed them into his fist, and passed the plate.

Pat Best does not know what financial arrangements, if any, were made later.

Tom Glaze, the chancellor, tells us about a young friend of his, Ashley Laser, who went down front with the children on Sunday morning for the young folks' sermon that the Presbyterians do so much good with.

Ashley is ten, and Judge Glaze describes her as being "very bright."

Here is how that inspiring moment went:

"The sermon was on tithing. The minister asked Ashley to hold out her hand and he placed ten animal cookies in her palm. He asked her to consider how many of the cookies she would return to him if she knew that she might receive a reward for her giving."

Ashley didn't have to consider at all. She gave all ten cookies back.

The minister was delighted and told the congregation, small and large, as much. That this young person would return all she had so that—he was in the process of saying when Ashley volunteered:

"I don't like animal cookies."

On the advice of a young friend sitting in the pew beside him, a five-year-old boy attending Park Hill Baptist Church merely thumped the bottom of the collection plate, letting it pass and holding onto his quarter offering.

"It didn't work," the youngster ruefully admitted to his granddad that evening.

Somebody saw?

Nobody saw. He got out of church with the quarter.

The trouble came in the afternoon when his mother found him with the quarter and he explained to her how you do the trick.

As Joey Beard, age eight, of Benton, changed out of his Sunday clothes, a quarter clunked from his pocket and rolled noisily across the floor.

Faye Beard, Joey's mother, made a nice pickup.

"Why, son, did you forget to give your offering at Sunday school?"

Joey said, no, he put in his offering.

In fact, he gave twice as much.

"You know my river money from Riverfest?"

Faye Beard knew that money.

"Well, I kept the measly quarter," Joey said, "and put in fifty cents' river money."

It was Krista Karnes, age four, who put her first quarter into the collection plate at Pine Bluff, and then demanded of the departing usher, "Well, what do we get?"

Not so Marc Crawley. Being six years old and the son of a minister, Marck knows his way around a church.

At First Baptist at Newport, Marc was sitting in the pew with his mother. Up front was Dad, the Rev. Gene Crawley.

Here came the collection plate.

Allison Crawley explains what happened.

"Mama had already announced that she left her purse at home and did not have the customary quarter. Marc was not going to be caught empty-handed."

Doubtless the minister's son was remembering the widow's mite. And Jesus' teaching that it matters not how much we give, but that we give of all we have.

"Marc dropped in a big wad of fuzz balls he pulled off of his sweater."

The Truth About Mothers

At Mother's Day church service, the little ones were down front for their visit with the pastor at Trinity United Methodist Church in Little Rock.

The Rev. William D. Elliott asked the children, "Now who can tell me, why do we have Mother's Day?"

An answer came immediately from a beautifully done-up little girl.

"Because of what mothers do to us!"

Moving on, Mr. Elliott asked the youngsters to share with him what some of the things were they had done that day especially for their mothers.

The minister called it quits after a small boy volunteered, "I cleaned up my room so there would be at least one clean room in the house."

The approach of Mother's Day reminds Honey Mitchell how grateful she is that no longer is there a Children's Day.

Not every town had a Children's Day.

Mrs. Mitchell's hometown, in Dallas County, practically could not wait for the occasion.

"They made me stand up every year and do the silliest things. Children's Day was the bane of my existence."

Mrs. Mitchell recalls with special anguish the year she stood up, laced and ruffled, and sang the soul-stirring song, "'Thout Mother" (Without Mother).

"I don't remember all the words, but this was a song about a family that was struggling along without a mother. I wasn't without my mother. She sat out in the audience while I stood up there making a fool of myself."

This is a verse from "'Thout Mother":

"Dear Papa does the best he can, but then you know he's just a man, and don't know how to fix and plan— 'thout Mother."

Mrs. Mitchell recalls that this went on, verse after verse, virtually without end.

"I know everybody thought I was a little tilted."

Finally, "'Thout Mother" ground along to the closing heart-tugging words.

"I was supposed to say that when this life is o'er we will go up to Heaven to Mother."

It didn't come out that way.

"I blew it, and sang we will go up to Heaven 'thout Mother."

From the way the audience exploded, it must have been worth all the pain.

The Dreaded Fun of Easter

As a youngster, she dreaded the fun of Easter.

Her church used the season for its big push, recruiting new young Christians.

A lady we know was remembering how it was thirty years ago in lower Pope County.

"The Saturday before Easter our church always had this big Easter egg hunt. Everybody got invited, but especially big old boys you never saw around the church any other time of the year."

The idea was that the big old boys would get caught up in the spirit of things and become young Christians.

She couldn't recall whose idea that was. Maybe the same elder who put on a Santa Claus suit and got his pockets picked at Christmas.

"Anyway, on Saturday morning before Easter, we all stayed home and dyed eggs in the kitchen."

The memory of hot vinegar stung her nose.

"You dyed your eggs so you could recognize them later. Maybe it was how the colors streaked and ran. Or how you put the little designs on."

She remembered pressing a decal of a flowery cross on a pale blue Easter egg, holding it beneath a wet cloth.

Things got folded up under there, and the flowery cross printed up like rabbit ears sticking out of a bush.

She could recognize that egg.

"You needed to know your own eggs, because after the hunt all the children got their eggs back, more or less."

Overhearing this, a fellow observed that he hadn't eaten a hardboiled egg since the Easter he was five years old. He remembered because that was the first year he got to wear long pants to the Easter egg hunt.

Also, that year he ate thirteen hardboiled eggs, which was about seven more than he could enjoy.

The last egg had been particularly green around the yolk. He had no idea how it got to the egg hunt, and more than fifty years later, did not care to speculate about it. At any rate, thirty years ago in lower Pope County, Saturday morning before Easter was spent dyeing eggs. Then in the afternoon everybody went to the church. The prospective young Christians were there early, not having brought any eggs.

Our narrator recalled:

"We turned all our eggs over to the adults, whoever the hiding committee was, and they hid the eggs."

Nobody peeped, except for the large visitors, who at that stage still were in the process of making up their minds about lifelong commitments.

Then an adult came back to where all the egg hunters were gathered and made informal remarks about see what a lot of fun we have in the youth activities of our church.

The propsective Christians heard none of this. Their eyes were glued to specific tree trunks and jonquil clusters and rock piles.

"Go!"

At "Go!" she always did one of two things.

Either she pretended to be thinking about something else or she contrived to trip over her own feet.

"With those bullies running around, my mother would have had to drag me to an egg and whip me before I'd have picked anything up."

Within minutes the prospective new Christians had virtually all the eggs rounded up and were back at the starting point, claiming whatever there was to claim for another year.

There was one exception.

She would always remember that just before each Easter egg hunt ended, the poorest child in town would somehow wander into the area of an encouraging adult and there—wonder of wonders!—find the biggest prize egg of all.

Remembering that, she loved Easter and she loved her church.

Epistles, Apostles, Possums, All In Howard's Hands

Everybody knows, or knew at some early age, the answer to that Sunday school question, "What are the epistles?"

At McGehee, it was a matter of whose hand shot up the fastest.

"Epistles, those were the wives of the Apostles."

The Rev. Larry D. Powell says we can forget that. Mr. Powell is pastor of Oaklawn United Methodist Church at Hot Springs.

"How many of you know what a possum is?"

That was Mr. Powell's question to the little ones gathered at the chancel Sunday for the Children's Sermon.

"A what?"

"A possum." The minister was eager to get on with it, to share the details of an encounter he'd had the previous week.

Several hands went up.

The microphone was steered to a youngster whose answer filled the sanctuary, "A possum is something like a disciple!"

It took a while for the worshipful roar to subside.

Mr. Powell explained to everybody that he had said "a possum," not "apostle."

And for the record, "An opossum is not related to an epistle, even by marriage."

But then, children hear what they hear.

The pastor at Oaklawn Methodist tells about a little girl who concluded her evening prayer by saying, "Goodnight, Howard."

It sounded like the early years of Monday Night Football.

The child's parents were puzzled. Flabbergasted was more like it.

One of them asked, "Who is Howard?"

The child was patient.

"Howard? That's God's name. Our Father who art in heaven, Howard be thy name."

Charles Bannerman of Hot Springs recalls a New York youngster's recitation of The Lord's Prayer: "Lead us not into Penn Station..."

When David Baker was growing up at Fordyce he had trouble making sense out of the scriptural passage always recited at the end of his Sunday school class.

Before dismissal, everybody stood and said, "Beat the doors of the world, but not Arizona."

Young David wondered why he couldn't beat the doors of Arizona, too.

That was some time ago. Lou Baker, who manages the Kings Inn at Camden, reports that now her son, the Rev. David Baker, has the passage sorted out.

He even used it in one of his early sermons, after entering the Methodist ministry:

"Be ye doers of the word, and not hearers only."

Matt Johnson was not similarly confused.

The Bible Church of Little Rock has fellowship meetings every other Wednesday night, and last time Dr. Bob Arrington, a deacon, held up a picture of the garden of Eden and asked four-year-old Matt to identify the scene.

Matt said, "It's the garden of Ethan Allen."

Dr. Arrington could understand a slip like that, what with television furniture sales going on.

The important thing was knowing the occupants of the garden.

"Who lived there?" he asked.

Matt Johnson said, "Allen and Eath."

A Cross-eyed Bear And A Palm-Leaf Fan

Next to the universally loved Round John Virgin, the most famous creature never to exist in all of religious music would have to be the cross-eyed bear.

Round John, as everybody knows who knows "Silent Night," is there in the manger every Christmas when little children sing about the mother and child, holy infant so limber and wild. Sleep is heavenly please.

The cross-eyed bear, on the other hand, has not been that well thought of at all.

Paul Meers, for one, remembers that when he was a child, the bear curled his hair with fright.

"This was at a brush arbor meeting in the woods up north of Batesville. I was about four years old and everybody started singing, 'The consecrated cross I'd bear.'"

That was scary enough, but simultaneously a woman in the congregation felt the power come over her.

"It was Aunt Sarah Jane," Meers says. "The minute everybody sang those words, Aunt Sarah let out one of her shouts, and I knew it was all over."

Meers remembers being scooped up by a protective grown cousin, at whom he kept shouting, "Where's that bear?"

It was a useful experience.

Many brush arbors later, young Paul was able to sit still when Aunt Sarah Jane went down to the front and started whamming his father on the head with her palm-leaf fan.

"My father was a dignified man. He wouldn't wear a collar and a tie, but he was a deacon and he sat down on the front row with the other deacons, a dignified man."

Under the power again, Aunt Sarah left her pew and started whopping Paul's daddy and shouting, "Walter

Meers, God bless those old gray hairs. Your mother has gone to glory and you'll go there too before long."

Paul Meers was especially proud of his daddy that day.

"It wasn't easy, being hit on the head and hollered at like that, but he stayed dignified."

A Tougher Audience Than Birds or Ferns

After retiring from a career in education, Tom E. Miller of Pine Bluff found himself at home in the role of househusband.

It did not work out in a rewarding way.

Alone for hours at a time, Miller wound up talking to himself. Also to family pets. And to ferns.

To get away from himself, Tom Miller went outside. There he tried to strike up conversations with birds. Some birds listened, but most flew away.

The last we heard, Miller was in a Pine Bluff grocery store. A little girl in a shopping cart told her mother, "That man's talking to the paper towels!"

That's when Tom Miller got into religion.

It is a pleasure to hear from him now, as pastoral administrator of St. Mary's Church at McGehee.

"Just a note to let you know how I am doing in my new occupation. The ministry certainly gives me enough opportunity to talk to people. There are times, though, when I wish I was back talking to the groceries."

Like the time at Vacation Bible School.

"The children had been studying the Ten Commandments, so I decided to see what they had learned."

Mr. Miller asked for a show of hands. "Can anyone give me one of the Commandments?"

Hands shot up.

"Thou shall not steal," a small boy said.

The pastoral administrator was gratified. "Good," he told the youngster. "Now can you explain what that means?"

The boy could explain and did.

"How about another Commandment?" Mr. Miller said.

Hands shot up.

"Honor thy father and thy mother."

Again he was pleased. "Very good. Can you tell me what that means? Honor thy father and thy mother?"

The little girl did a good job.

No time to stop now.

"How about another Commandment, please?" Mr. Miller challenged.

A small girl blurted, "Thou shall not commit adultery."

"Yes," Mr. Miller declared, "and how about another Commandment?"

Mrs. Miller had to sympathize with her husband.

"When I told this story to my wife, she remembered an incident that occurred in her Sunday school class years ago. We were living in Florida at the time."

Among all the fruit trees.

With her sixth-grade class, Mrs. Miller was discussing human growth and maturation.

One of the youngsters asserted that he already had reached maturity.

Mrs. Miller said, well, probably not.

"She decided to explain the meaning of maturity, using the orange tree as an example."

Take the orange blossom.

"We can look at the blossom as the stage of infancy." Then the small green fruit. "With fruit itself, we move from infancy to late childhood." Next the larger fruit, almost grown, but yet unripe. "There we see adolescence." And finally, the large ripe orange.

"I know, I know," a youngster interrupted the narrative. "That's adultery!"

A Running Start on Faith

A friend in Iowa has sent to Mrs. Mae Henderson of Little Rock a newspaper clipping detailing the amazing ability of an eleven-year-old girl to stand up and say the Bible.

The girl got up at church one night two weeks ago, it was a little after 7 o'clock, and started in saying the Bible.

She was still standing there saying it at 8:55 when the congregation got up and went home, convinced.

Possibly she is still standing there. At a quarter to 10, the weekly newspaper reporter herself got up and left.

Mrs. Mae Henderson says:

"According to the reporter, this little girl talks so fast you cannot always tell which part of the Bible she is reciting, and she does not recite in any particular order. Apparently there is no end to how long she could keep it up."

Such feats are certainly possible.

We knew a girl in the second grade at McGehee, sat not two feet from her, who could get up and say all the books of the Bible in five seconds. That's not the same as getting up and saying the whole Bible, but this girl was still four years short of eleven.

Fast was the only way she could recite the books. If she tried to go slow, it took her five minutes of turning red to recite the title to Leviticus by itself:

"Levik—I mean...

"Leviki—wait a minute...

"LeVIKitus!"

But going fast, she was amazing. Not that anybody understood a word she said. It could have been two-all-beef-patties-special-sauce-lettuce-cheese-pickles-onions-on-a-sesame-seed-bun. Except that everybody knew this girl's daddy was a preacher of some sort, his church being somewhere out in suburban McGehee. About six miles out. Past Bayou Bartholomew.

Such a feat would be even more amazing if a person didn't get up and achieve it three times a week.

Faith is the most powerful thing there is.

As a youngster, we had a straight pin on the head of which was inscribed the Lord's Prayer.

Or maybe it was the New Testament. We owned the pin personally.

No, the naked eye could not make out the actual writing on the pinhead. Neither could any other kind of earthly eye.

But by turning the pin at just the right angle, out in the bright sunlight, a person could get an idea of what the man in the carnival was talking about.

Here is what the carnival man said, standing there in his booth next to the shooting gallery, offering to make the religious pin available:

"Yes, you boys can shoot them guns. Or you can go over there and pay your money and dip for them fish. But as Paul said in his letter to the Epistles, he who does not love the Lord's word and His treasures will burn in Hell for all of infinity. Do any of you boys have any idea how long infinity is?"

Everybody didn't.

"Infinity is how long it would take for a sparrow's wing to wear away the earth if the earth was a steel ball and the sparrow flew by once every ten thousand years. And that's only the beginning of how long a person would burn in Hell!"

The amazing thing was that he would part with this religious treasure for only a dime. Or at a special group rate, three straight pins for a quarter.

Why God Created Fleas

We Personally Have Nothing Against Brokella

Some days ago the good people of Pottsville ate a dinner in honor of Boyce Sinclair.

The dinner was served in the basement of the Associate Reformed Presbyterian Church, where "Mr. Boyce" has been a member for something like eighty-nine years.

The ladies of Pottsville are wonderful cooks. We recommend the basement of the ARP Church as being a good place to eat, although it is not open at all times. Sometimes they are down there quilting.

Five broccoli casseroles were brought to this special meal. Or maybe it was ten broccoli casseroles.

Something needs to be said about this.

Ten years ago nobody had ever thought about broccoli.

We heard a woman ask the produce manager in a grocery store, "What is this green thing?"

The produce manager said, "That's some of that new brokella."

"Brokella?"

"That's something like what you call it."

The woman put the green thing down. "Well I don't want any of it."

The produce man said, "I'm with you, ma'am."

But now, overnight, broccoli is on everybody's lips. And down everybody's shirt fronts.

Ten broccoli casseroles are brought to a church dinner for Boyce Sinclair.

Or maybe it was fifteen broccoli casseroles.

We asked the honoree about it.

"I haven't eaten any that I know of," Mr. Boyce said, referring to the twenty broccoli casseroles.

He is a gentle man, with a large capacity for gratitude, and did not want to make a point of it.

"I think the ladies have done a very nice job," Mr. Boyce said. "Very wonderful."

Yes, and they are doing a wonderful job in church basements throughout Little Rock. And Dumas. And Paragould and Fort Smith and Texarkana. Nine out of ten church ladies have taken on broccoli as their own personal specialty.

Listen to this.

Broccoli is not mentioned in the Bible.

"I think you would be safe in saying that," John Workman, an ordained minister, told us.

Neither is broccoli with mushroom soup and almonds.

Nor broccoli with Sugar Frosted Flakes.

Somebody has to get up and say something before it's too late.

Although for our part, personally, we have nothing against this vegetable, if that is what it is.

In fact, pass some more of that brokella, please.

Something About Godliness and Cleanliness, Wasn't It?

The spaghetti was disgusting in appearance. Sickening brown. And the taste would have gagged a goat. Don A. Travis, son of the Rev. Donald Travis, pastor of Lawson Baptist Church, has the queasy details.

A mission team from Lawson Baptist went north to teach Christian love and kindness to some people in Indiana. It's a good thing they didn't go to give cooking lessons.

The problem began when Johnny Crossley volunteered to cook a spaghetti dinner for the mission crew.

Crossley prepared the dinner, then left instructions for the final step with two twelve-year-old girls.

"Watch the spaghetti," Crossley directed, referring to the pasta in the boiling water.

Came dinner time, and the mission team sat down to eat. That first bite after saying the blessing. It made everybody's eyes water.

That second bite. Forget the second bites.

As grateful as the missionaries were, they made quick work of abandoning the meal.

Don Travis explains, "It was concluded that somebody had purchased a package of really bad spaghetti."

The return trip home from Indiana to South Arkansas was uneventful.

Well, there was one event. The spaghetti mystery was solved.

One of the twelve-year-old girls told the Rev. Donald Travis that she and the other girl did exactly as instructed by Johnny Crossley.

"We washed the spaghetti, just like he said."

Mr. Travis, knowing some persons do rinse their pasta, reacted jokingly. "Did you wash it in Ajax?"

The girl replied in a serious tone. "No, I believe it was Dove."

Beware of Methodists on Culinary Adventures

In October the Methodist Men of Blytheville began a series of eating adventures at their monthly dinner meetings.

The first meal wasn't all that daring.

L.D. (Buck) Harris describes the menu:

"Soul food was served for the October meeting, including turnips, greens, white beans, and corn pone."

In November the action picked up.

"The menu featured lamb fries, which were devoured with gusto—some even went back for seconds. One naive member wondered beforehand, 'Do they taste like lamb chops?' Another said, 'Just what do they taste like?' and received the proper answer: 'Compared to what?'"

December's dinner has created suspense.

"The menu will feature wild duck," Buck Harris says. "That is, if the ace duck hunters in the group (including myself) can bag a few limits. I hunted the first day of the season and didn't even see a limit fly over, much less bag a limit."

Then the Methodist Men of Blytheville will begin a new year. Or that is the hope, anyway.

"The January meeting will feature coon and sweet taters, with the ace coon hunters supplying the food."

Menus are not planned beyond January. Harris explains why.

"Group leaders will need to see how many members they have run off."

Church Members
Stalled By Beer

At a beer display in the Kroger store on Cantrell Road, Bill Joe Carpenter ran into a lady from his church.

The beer was marked with a reduced price and Carpenter was about to put a couple of six-packs into his shopping cart.

When the lady from the church wheeled up, Carpenter thought better of it.

They talked awhile.

Then they talked some more.

The woman made no move in any direction.

"We talked about Easter and the church egg hunt and a half a dozen other things. Finally I excused myself and pushed on down the aisle."

After a few feet, Carpenter turned around to see whether it was safe to go back and get beer.

It was, because the church friend was just pushing around the corner. With four six-packs.

Conscientiousness in the marketplace is to be admired.

Neither man who was there will forget the young woman who took their order when they sat down for lunch at a Little Rock country club.

One man was in the garb of a Roman Catholic clergyman.

The waitress had just arrived on the job.

They told her, "Before we eat, we're going to have a libation."

She closed her eyes and bowed her head.

Must Be Time for Church

Watches give out all sorts of information.

We were visiting on a downtown sidewalk with a friend who suddenly became nervous.

Looking up the street, he said, "Uh-oh, here comes my preacher."

Our friend twitched, but there was no escaping into daylight.

The minister approached, smiling warmly. "Hi, Phil. We've been missing you."

Phil shook hands and said, "You bet. I have too. I mean, I haven't been missing me. But you just wouldn't believe how busy the weekends have been."

The minister, having only a minute, said he understood.

"Will we be seeing you Sunday?" He said this moving away.

Phil looked at his wrist watch. Absurdly. Then just as quickly he put his arm down. "Yes, I'll be able to make it."

At mid-afternoon on Tuesday, Phil's wrist watch told him he would be able to make church Sunday.

The minister was gone, and our friend felt like a fool. "Why did I do that?"

He swore at his own moral impotence.

But the watch was right. And now Phil hasn't missed in four straight Sundays.

Miracle on Fourche Bayou

Robert Moore, the younger, served as pastor at Highland Methodist Church in Little Rock.

One of his flock was B. Frank Mackey, then Pulaski County sheriff.

One afternoon, the preacher was invited to go on the sheriff's rounds.

They drove out beyond Fourche Bayou and turned into the woods.

"After about 100 yards or so the road became almost impassable."

Sheriff Mackey was turning the car around when a man appeared out of the woods.

The man had a keg on his shoulder.

Sheriff Mackey muttered to Dr. Moore, "I thought so. Watch this."

The sheriff hit his flashing light switch and turned on the siren.

He stepped out of the car.

The man with the keg stopped. He put his burden gently down on the ground.

Sheriff Mackey said, "All right, Jake. What is all this about?"

Jake's face became animated.

"Why sheriff, we're having a revival meeting down here. And I'm being the water boy."

Preacher Moore watched as the sheriff drew out his large pistol.

"He knocked the cork out of the keg. He stuck his finger into the opening, then to his tongue."

The sheriff said, "Jake, stick your finger in there. Then you tell me that keg's full of water."

Jake did as ordered.

His face became radiant.

"Sheriff," he said, withdrawing his finger from his mouth. "The good Lord has done it again!"

A Little Help Doesn't Hurt

The flowers are here, all around the square, because of a united effort by Fayetteville merchants.

All growing things are identified with small name tags planted alongside.

Browse here in the herb garden, next to The Old Post Office Restaurant in the center of the square.

Sage, rosemary, thyme—no parsley?—oregano, dill, basil, woodruff (woodruff?), tarragon, sweet marjoram.

"It is really one of the nicest things that Fayetteville has ever done."

The speaker is a tall, young man, explaining the flowers to two women who are leading a man and a boy.

The young man wears a blue shoulder satchel, and a beard of almost matching color.

He adds with pride, "I believe Fayetteville is growing up."

The women agree that the setting is beautiful.

One says, "Who does the actual work?"

The young man thinks, and then replies, "It is a project of the businessmen. But I believe God does the actual work."

The Excuses of the Fisherman

Randy Lindsey of Mena tells about a youngster who showed up late for Sunday school.

The teacher wanted an explanation.

"I was going fishing," the boy said, "but my daddy wouldn't let me."

The Sunday school teacher was delighted.

"You're fortunate to have such a fine father. Did he explain to you why you shouldn't go fishing on Sunday?"

The boy said yes'm.

"He said there wasn't enough bait for both of us."

Randy Lindsey has his own position on the subject.

"My grandmother (bless her heart) threatened all forms of disaster—from lightning striking to drowning—as punishment for fishing on Sunday.

"She never really favored my rationalization that the fish were being punished for trying to steal worms on Sunday."

Why God Created Fleas

Warren Wilhite of Sherwood is grateful to his cousin down in Louisiana for identifying the origin of fleas.

By legislative enactment, Louisiana has an official dog. The catahoula hound. Maybe that's why they know so much about fleas.

His cousin down there notified Warren Wilhite that God created the earth and all in it in six days, rested the seventh, and on the eighth day found Adam and his dog asleep in the shade of a tree when they should have been rounding up the other animals and naming them.

"God saw that this was not good. He took some hairs from the dog's back and changed them into fleas so the dog could get no rest."

That wasn't all.

"Then God took one of Adam's ribs, and from it made a woe-man. Called her Eve."

Wilhite contends, or his cousin does, that from that day to this, man has not rested either.

Our associates Sue Harvey and Mary Beth Henderson have studied the Wilhite explanation, which cites the Bible to show God created fleas and women (in that order) to keep dogs and their masters from getting any sleep under shade trees.

Harvey and Henderson observe:

"We found this explanation of the existence of our gender to be almost amusing, although not terribly accurate.

"As we understand the logic, it goes thus: Men are lazy, men need woe, therefore, God created—fleas?

"Shouldn't fleas be called woe-dogs?

"And, if there be no fleas and no women, would males be woebegone?"

Teen-agers Up To No Good? No? Good.

Strange cars began arriving at the Little Rock residence shortly before 7:30 p.m. It was Wednesday evening.

The family was away on vacation—neighbors were aware of that—and yet these cars kept coming, young men in their late teens getting out and going into the house.

It didn't take a genius to recognize the makings of some wild goings-on.

One of the neighbors stood it only so long.

He went to the front door and demanded entry and an explanation.

Inside, it turned out that the main culprit was Mike Sells. A sophomore-to-be at Hendrix College, Sells was house-sitting for the owners.

His group gathered there, or he would have missed the meeting.

So, caught red-handed sitting around the living room were twelve to fifteen members of Young Life, a non-denominational student religious group.

They were having their Bible study.

Alone again, the Young Lifers had a huge laugh.

"Everybody knows," somebody said, "that a bunch of teen-agers never get together unless something rotten is going on."

It is the unremitting irony. Nobody knows so well as the teen-agers, themselves, that the assertion simply is not true.

But the group did acknowledge something else about the neighbor.

"You have to admire the courage it took for him to come over here."

Religious activity is not always what it appears to be.

We recall just after the Supreme Court's ruling on prayer that two youngsters were found on their knees in the back of a school room.

The principal stormed at them, "What are you two doing down there?"

One youngster said, "We're shooting craps."

The principal calmed down. "Well, all right then, go ahead. I thought for a minute you two were praying."

Maybe that is not a good example.

Our growing up in McGehee was of religious bent.

Most of one summer we broke into the church every night.

Some would say it was to get at the tumbling mats in the church basement.

Some would say, in fact, that there was not a religious bone in those culprit bodies flopping around down there after dark.

One of our group, compelled to name two books of the Bible, came up with "Dude 'n' Romany."

His brother provided, "First and Second Philippinos."

It kept up most of one summer, the religious breaking and entering, until one night, Rev. John Hefley joined the group, coming in unannounced through the same window.

Brother Hefley recited some pertinent commandments, unheard of until that moment. The next Sunday, everybody had the honor of sitting down front in the first pew.

Dude 'n' Romany stood up, faced the congregation and sang, "Everything's All Right in My Father's House."

Blue Laws and Moral Uplift

Suddenly, after all these years, you can buy anything in the house on Sunday.

We recall days of going into the Terri Lynn Store on Cantrell Road, trying to buy cabbage for hot dog slaw, something fancy for Sunday.

"I can't sell you cabbage," Harry Giberson would say, "but I can sell you lettuce."

Then he would think a minute. "Or maybe it's the other way around."

You had to get out the list to remember which was moral—cabbage or lettuce.

The Sunday Laws uplifted people in various ways.

We knew one grocery store, not Harry Giberson's, where customers regularly went on Sunday, picked up what they wanted and put it down on the counter.

The proprietor would say, "I can't sell you that today."

The customer would say, "I bought it yesterday and forgot to take it with my other things."

The proprietor would say, "When you bought it yesterday, did you remember to leave the money for it?"

The customer would say, "No, I forgot that too."

Whereupon the customer was permitted to do the moral thing, correct his oversight, and be on his way.

A woman we know thinks the demise of Blue Laws promises a dramatic increase in church attendance.

If people have been telling the truth.

"Half the women I know say the reason they couldn't make it was because they couldn't find a decent pair of panty hose."

Panty hose were among those things that could not be bought on Sunday.

"Now you can pick them up on the way to services."

The Lord Probably Loves Texans, Too

Some people say Razorback football is a religion in Arkansas.

Twenty years ago, the Rev. Andrew Hall clarified the matter with a sign he put outside the First Baptist Church in Fayetteville.

That sign at the church said, "Football Is Only A Game. Eternal Things Are Spiritual. Nevertheless— BEAT TEXAS."

A Clarendon woman put her husband in the hospital at Stuttgart last weekend for some tests.

Labor Day turned up and delayed the results until Tuesday.

It made for a long wait.

Some relatives appeared on Sunday. One of them said, "We'll all be praying tomorrow night."

The wife appreciated this concern. Family prayers during the last hours before getting the results.

The relative went on.

"Because we're going to need all the prayers we can get to beat Texas."

Before moving to Little Rock to become senior minister at Pulaski Heights United Methodist Church, Dr. Gerald R. Mullikin preached in Texas.

Sunday morning Dr. Mullikin reflected with a beaming countenance on the downpour outside.

"The Lord is blessing us with this badly needed rain."

And there was something else to beam about.

The minister noted that the afternoon before, Saturday afternoon, the Arkansas Razorbacks were down in Austin for a football game.

He told his congregation, "Throughout the weeks before this game, I was on the telephone with people I know, preachers down in Texas."

Dr. Mullikin was not prepared to elaborate.

But he did want to make an announcement.

"I can tell you this morning that in the days ahead several contributions will be coming up from Texas to this church."

He added, "If you know what I mean."

When the laughter died, he said, "And I see that you do know what I mean."

Frank and Wilma Morrison of Little Rock attended church in suburban Dallas one Sunday, going there with friends.

It happened to be the Sunday after a fine Razorback romp with the Longhorns.

The proceedings were relaxed, reminding Frank Morrison of his early church days in Johnson County.

"Back then when somebody visited church, everybody gathered around and tried to take him home to Sunday dinner."

Morrison sensed that feeling in Dallas when the minister took registration cards from the collection plate to acknowledge the presence of visitors.

He got to the Morrisons' card last.

"We have with us also a couple from Little Rock."

The minister paused.

"That's in Arkansas."

He paused again.

"I know that at the end of the service our congregation will want to greet most of our visitors, bearing in mind that on this particular morning the Christian spirit cannot be expected to extend itself to people from the state of Arkansas.

"Bear also in mind that I'll be down here in front with you at that time, and as a graduate of the University of Texas, I'll be taking names."

Genuine 9 Indian Fruit Oil

While David and Geneva Bentley toured the aisles at the Wal-Mart store, outfitting themselves for a trip to Missouri, their son David more or less followed them around.

David Bentley is not a toddler.

He is, in fact, the Rev. David B. Bentley, campus minister at Arkansas State University.

"Following someone around Wal-Mart is not the highest form of entertainment," observes Mr. Bentley, "so I was reading labels on aerosol cans to add to the excitement of the occasion."

He was not prepared for what he found.

"My eyes were drawn to an odd-looking can with an Indian chief's head and a cornucopia on the label."

The minister allowed himself to be drawn even closer.

Readers who cannot handle real excitement are warned not to proceed further.

David Bentley got himself close enough to the Indian's head and the cornucopia to read the aerosol can:

"GENUINE 9 INDIAN FRUIT OIL, MONEY BLESSING OFFERING SPRAY, INDIAN SPIRIT."

The minister did not holler for his parents, but he did have sense enough to take a step backward.

"The front label did not tell me what I had found."

He stepped forward again and spun the can around.

"The reverse label was in Spanish, which means nothing to someone who studied New Testament Greek."

Unflinching, David Bentley picked up the can and found the directions.

Here is how to use Genuine 9 Indian Fruit Oil purchased in the Wal-Mart store in Jonesboro:

"Shake well. Hold can upright and point nozzle away from you. Press button down to spray. Aim upwards and spray all areas of your surroundings. Repeat spraying as necessary. Let us pray. Make the sign of the cross. Air freshener deodorizer. Does not have supernatural powers."

Naturally we wasted no time beating it out to one of Mr. Sam's stores at Little Rock, the Wal-Mart at West Markham Street.

"Do what?" the young clerk asked, herself taking a step backward.

We explained it again. Genuine 9 Indian Fruit Oil. The product with the money house blessing, although it lacks supernatural powers.

"Excuse me," the young clerk said. "I'll get my manager."

She retreated down the aisle and disappeared to the right and left simultaneously.

That was Thursday. Since then we have seen nothing of her or her manager.

It is apparent that Mr. Sam's Little Rock people have not yet acquired the sophistication to handle Genuine 9 Indian Fruit Oil.

Several of our more elegant readers are asking how they might get hold of some Genuine 9 Indian Fruit Oil.

No reader is more elegant than Bayard Phillips of Choctaw.

"I would give up to $3 for a quart of something like that."

He means a quart of what is called by its full name Genuine 9 Indian Fruit Oil, Money Blessing Offering Spray, Indian Spirit.

Small wonder that Bayard Phillips is interested.

"Besides living at Choctaw, I am told of having some Indian connections in the family, namely my great-aunt Phyllis was a full-blooded halfbreed."

This gives Phillips assurance when he wanders too far from his retirement home at the western end of Greers Ferry Lake.

"Out in the woods, I have trouble with directions. Frankly, I probably would panic if it was not for my heritage."

The last Indian we heard of named Phillips was a utility infielder for Cleveland. He hit like his name might have been Phyllis.

But not everybody is familiar with Genuine 9 Indian Fruit Oil.

According to the directions, Genuine 9 Indian Fruit Oil has no supernatural powers. Don't bet the parsonage on that.

"My wife and I were on our way home from a vacation and we decided to stop in Russellville to see my brother, who was a coach at the high school at the time."

This testimonial comes from another man of the cloth, from Tom Hazelwood, Methodist minister at Tyronza.

Roaming through the house at Russellville, Mr. Hazelwood came on a spray can with an Indian head on it.

He received a caution.

"My brother warned me to be careful and not waste any of the spray."

Church leaders are only human. Most of them.

"You would think a minister would be able to resist temptation. But I was only a youth director in El Dorado at the time."

Tom Hazelwood took the can of Genuine 9 and went off by himself.

"As a Methodist, I am not sure how I figured out how to do it, but I sprayed the sign of the cross."

The first thing everybody did was run out of the house.

After an interval, a volunteer went in and turned on the exhaust fan.

Then Tom Hazelwood's brother gathered up all of the towels in sight and took them to the washing machine.

Not long after that, the minister and his wife, Stephanie, found themselves driving south out of Russellville.

"Our van broke down in Conway."

Now for the money blessing.

"The tow and repair bill came to about $350. I could have had the same thing done for about $150 in El Dorado."

Mr. Hazelwood accepted the bill stoically.

"I did not tell the Conway garage manager why he had received this blessing."

Each person must discover the answer.

"While there may be a money blessing, and you may be involved in it, there is no guarantee that you will be on the receiving end."

Bound For Glory

At Fort Smith, in his 80th year, Ray Vandiver rides the church bus to Sunday services. Vandiver stopped driving last year.

His wife, sixty, has taken up driving for the first time. But Vandiver has been nowhere with Mrs. Vandiver behind the wheel.

They say admiringly throughout the congregation, "Mr. Van prefers the fellowship of the church bus. He thinks it's a perfect way to begin a day of worship."

With two Sundays to go in 1980, and Ray Vandiver's perfect attendance record on the line, a telephone call came to the house.

The regular bus driver was leaving town on short notice. Worshippers would have to get to Sunday school and church the best ways they could.

Vandiver said wait a minute.

Could the bus be brought to his house?

The driver said, "Well, Mr. Van, I guess so."

That was done. Through a minor miracle, the church bus ran as usual, with all regular riders picked up on time.

At Sunday school, somebody proposed a resolution commending Mrs. Vandiver.

"What for?" Mrs. Vandiver said.

"For getting everybody here."

But then one of the bus riders stood up and explained.

"It was Mr. Van who drove us here. He said if he was going to meet his Maker, it wasn't going to be with his eyes closed."

Harold Davidson was driving the bus for Trinity United Methodist Church at North Little Rock.

Davidson's assistant driver was Mark Shelby, age five, whose main responsibility was opening the bus door.

As they drove in the Rose City area, young Mark asked the man behind the wheel, "Will this bus be in Heaven?"

Harold Davidson says he struggled to control the bus. Then he felt a need to be positive and encouraging.

"If God feels we could use this bus in Heaven and it would bless people, I think it will be there."

The youngster said, "How will it get there?"

Davidson said, well, the bus would be lifted, just raised right up from the earth, like all the good people on hand when the time came.

Mark gave that serious consideration, then said he had a better idea.

"I want us to drive it."

Being assistant driver on the Trinity bus is educational.

Bill McCord was driving that same bus with a young assistant, age five, named Kenneth.

Harold Davidson describes the situation.

"It had just come a big rain, and on Highway 161 at Protho Junction the highway was covered with water at a railroad underpass."

Bill McCord stopped the bus at the water's edge, opened the door and told Kenneth:

"The assistant driver has to wade through the water to see how deep it is, and see if the bus can make it."

Kenneth stood up and turned, walking down the aisle toward the back of the bus.

"Get you another assistant," he said. "I quit."

Dogwoods And Him

In a country churchyard we asked some ladies directions.

They were seeing to the grounds, picking up whatever the week had blown there from the crossroads.

And admiring all over again the Lord's handiwork.

"Oh yes, we put them out," one of the ladies said, surveying the profusion of bulbs, the brilliant reds and yellows, the waves of forsythia and japonica.

And the double crowns, two dogwood trees.

"We put them out, but we all know who made them look like this."

She laughed that anybody would take credit otherwise.

This sister of the church and one other—she sat there in the smock with lavender pockets—as little girls, they hunted Easter eggs on these very grounds. Their daughters came along and did the same thing. Now, just a few days ago, their grandchildren brought baskets, although one slept through it on her granddaddy's shoulder.

"These dogwoods, now we did not put these trees out."

She said they had never been more beautiful.

"But of course they will never get any bigger. Not with Him crucified that way."

It is a stunning thing to move through life seeing the whole picture, then on the verge of reaching maturity itself to be handed a missing piece.

Christ crucified on a cross of dogwood.

Confronted by incomprehension, the woman in the country churchyard turned away and busied herself with wisps of scrap paper and a collapsed can, Miller Lite.

There is no telling what you might catch from strangers eaten up with religious ignorance.

We put it to a friend, a man of the cloth.

He said, "Oh, yes."

Oh, yes, what?

"Oh, yes, a lot of people say that's how it happened."

The volume is called *The Christian Book of WHY.*

It addresses all sorts of questions about why certain people believe as they believe, and do as they do.

On Page 228 is the question, "Why is the dogwood tree a symbol of Jesus' crucifixion?"

Here is the explanation:

"According to a legend which began as early as the second century, the dogwood tree was the size of the mighty oak and other trees of the forest until the time of Jesus' crucifixion. The timber of the dogwood was so firm and strong that it was chosen for the cross of Jesus. God, then, cursed the tree so that it would never again grow large enough to be used for such a cruel purpose."

That was not all of it.

"On that day, according to the same tradition, the dogwood tree became slender, bent, and twisted and its blossoms had two long and two short petals in the form of a cross. In the center of each petal's outer edge were nail prints, brown with rust and stained blood-red. A crown of thorns was at the flower's outer edge to remind the faithful throughout history of the curse of the dogwood."

It is quite all right, a minister assured us, that we should have been confused about the dogwood tree.

It is also all right, he said, that the good woman in Howard County turned away rather than risk unsavory association.

The minister said, "Some believers are more certain of their facts than others."

An Undertaking of Some Kind

In the shadow of the enormous statue, Christ of the Ozarks, some tourists from Kansas are puzzling over the language of a sign that advertises the Passion Play.

The sign says whatever your travel plans are, cancel them. One must stay to see a performance of the Passion Play.

It is the best undertaking of its kind, the sign says, since Christ Himself was on earth. Performances are nightly ($4 to $7) at the giant outdoor theater.

The cast features actual camels, donkeys, and primitive dogs. It is the primitive dogs that worry the folks from Kansas.

"What do you suppose those are?" the woman says.

Her husband is reading the sign with his arms folded.

"It could be those dogs with a pointy face that's close to the ground and not much ears."

The woman looks at the sign. She wonders what's to keep a primitive dog, right in the middle of the Passion Play, from chewing on somebody's robe. Just ripping it right off.

Something else concerns her husband.

"What's to keep a primitive dog from forgetting the play and running up in the stands where the people are? Even a plain smart dog might do that."

The woman reads the words again, aloud. "Primitive dogs." She cannot take it beyond that.

Entering the gate, tourists approach the statue from behind.

A man and woman have entered, getting out of an Oklahoma car, and he has stopped to take a piture.

The man is leaning back, aiming the camera sharply upward. It is said to be seven floors high, up there at the top. The photographer is almost falling over backward.

"What are you doing?" his wife says.

"I'm taking a picture."

She says, lowering her voice, "That's the back of it."

He says, "Oh," and takes the camera down.

They walk around to the front side.

The man says, "Boy, that is really something."

She says he doesn't have to talk that loud.

The man says, "I'll bet the shadow on the ground weighs a hundred pounds itself."

His wife says he had better shut up talking like that.

It is Sunday morning.

A teen-aged girl is reading from a folder. At her side is a boy, about ten, looking up at the statue. The boy is drinking a Shasta.

"It weighs more than a million pounds of concrete."

The boy wants to know who said so. Who weighed the statue?

The girl goes on reading. "You could hang a car from either arm and it wouldn't bother the statue."

The boy says, aw, you couldn't do that. He backs away, still looking up.

"The statue would withstand a wind of five hundred miles an hour."

The boy says, aw, it wouldn't either. Not five hundred miles an hour.

His sister quits reading and snaps, "They wouldn't lie about this." Feeling the presence of others, she lowers her voice. "They wouldn't lie."

The boy is chastized. He comes back and stands close to her.

"Maybe you could hang a car," he says, "but I bet you couldn't hang a station wagon."

We were not able to photgraph the Christ of the Ozarks.

Something was not right about the angle. Or the bright sunlight. Our finger would not push the button.

With another camera, on request, we photographed the Kansas couple, those folks who had not sorted out their thoughts about primitive dogs.

They stood at the base of the statue. In the foreground there will be a Shasta can.

Signs and
Wonders

Pay Now, Sin Later

The editorial was headlined "The need for a 'Fellowship of the Fallen.'"

It proposed a new beginning for religious leaders who get themselves defrocked, largely by defrocking themselves to begin with.

Repentance would be the thing.

The editorial came to this assertion:

"The prepentance of one sinner causes more joy in heaven than 99 just persons who require no rejuvenation."

Prepentance.

Pay in advance!

Charlie Hyatt of Jonesboro is fascinated by the potential.

Untold numbers of persons might catch fire with it.

"I am intrigued," Charlie Hyatt declares, "by the possibilities of prepentance. Until I read the Gazette editorial, I assumed that repentance could only follow one's transgressions."

But see what has happened.

"You have opened up a whole new approach to sin—an approach I find very appealing. I see now, although Webster hasn't gotten the word, that for those who plan ahead, there is a better way. If you pay in advance (expressions of guilt, sorrow and regret) for actions you are about to take, you can get the agony over with. This leaves you free to relax and enjoy yourself with none of the bad after-effects.

"This is a big improvement over the system I've been using. Thanks for the tip."

We talked with the writer of the editorial.

He said no one could have been more astonished than he, when he got up the next morning and read "the prepentance of one sinner" instead of what he set out to write, "the repentance of one sinner."

"I knew right away I had invented an important word."

Was it an accident, an ordinary typo? Or was this something larger? He could not say.

There is on record a case of prepentance in Arkansas. Actually, a partial payment.

"There was this revival at Ola," a man told us. "A woman went down front and confessed to just about everything."

Not holding back, the sinner acknowledged, "Yes, I have run with the men!"

Large intaking of congregational breath.

"And, yes! I have drainked the whiskey."

A larger gasp still.

"And, yes. I have gambled at cards."

Was there no end to the dreadful list?

"But praise the Lord!" the sinner shouted, in a voice audible across half of Yell County. "Praise the Lord, I've almost quit!"

Signs Make Several Wonder

Dan Morris and his family encountered a van on Petit Jean Mountain.

Lettering on the side said "Pentecostal Pest Control." Dan Morris didn't know which way to go with it.

"I mean, is this a service offered by the Pentecostal folks, controlling pests? Or is it some Baptists trying to keep the Pentecostal folks themselves in check?"

Gayle Windsor saw the sign en route to Mena, on the roadside west of Mount Ida: Little Hope Baptist Church.

Windsor says:

"This must be a new branch of the denomination, although doctrinally out of step with most Baptist sects."

On a trip to western Arkansas we saw this sign at an aging roadside house of worship near the southern border of Scott County: GRENADE HOLINESS CHURCH

That will get your attention.

Carl E. Barnes of Fairview United Methodist Church in Camden has a matter that might be considered by the church board.

It's a matter of two signs.

"One sign," Carl Barnes reports, "says 'Fairview United Methodist Church—A Warm and Loving Church.'"

A few inches away, near some air conditioning equipment, a second sign instructs, "KEEP OUT."

Wanda Laughon of Fairfield Bay has another sign that may be intimidating. She found it in a newspaper she gets regularly from Wichita Falls, Texas.

The warning sign is at a parking lot owned by the Messiah Lutheran Church: MESSIAH PARKING ONLY.

Anybody but the Lord Himself gets towed away.

The Oldsmobile on the cafeteria parking lot was new, dark blue.

"Really a nice looking car," says Larry Powell. "But that was not what caught our attention."

The Powells pulled in nose-to-nose with a personalized license plate.

"You know the kind. HIS, HERS, OURS, JIMMY, BEULAH, 007, SLIM, CHICK, PAID-4, whatever."

But not this Arkansas tag.

This tag on the cafeteria parking lot said: JESUS.

Larry Powell is a Methodist minister.

Looking at the tag, he felt himself beginning to have silly thoughts.

What silly thoughts will a man confess to?

"For one thing, I've actually wondered about what kind of car Jesus would drive if He were on earth now. And would He have a personalized license plate?"

Larry and Terri Powell went inside.

"Once inside the cafeteria, we scanned the serving line and dining room to see if anybody looked like, well, if anybody looked like he or she went with that particular car. No one stood out. Like I said, the whole thing got silly."

And it got sillier still.

"And then we wondered, Terri and I did, that if 'He' was in the area but NOT eating in that particular eatery, then what did that suggest about this cafeteria?"

Already in line, the Powells did not back out.

"Somehow it did seem appropriate that if an earthly residence was gong to be assumed, Arkansas would be the logical choice."

We will not know the answer to that one, probably for a while.

As for the personalized tag, well...

"The owner of the vehicle may have been a retired baseball player of Mexican descent, or perhaps a local Christian trying to make a social statement."

Larry Powell set aside his wondering and ate. But only after wondering this:

"I also wondered some other things (far too many to mention). Things like, would Jesus own a theme park? Would He preach in a Crystal Cathedral? Would He have a church at all, or would He just go from door to door?"

One thing Mr. Powell didn't wonder.

"The singer, Ray Stevens, has already asked the musical question, 'Would Jesus wear a Rolex?' I think that one has been pretty well settled."

If You'll Direct Your Attention to the Bulletin...

From the weekly bulletin of Highland Valley United Methodist Church in Little Rock:

> *NEW CHURCH COOKBOOK*
> *Circle No. 6 is producing a new cookbook*
> *with your assistance and the help of God.*

Finally, a way to get rid of those broccoli casseroles.

From the June 5, 1988, bulletin at Cabot United Methodist Church:

> *WANTED: A 3 Yr. Old Teacher on Monday*
> *and Wednesday, 8:30 to 1:30.*

Our correspondent wishes to remain anonymous.
But she does disclose this: "The preacher says the way it's going, a three-year-old might have to be hired."

And from the *Circuit-Writer,* a weekly bulletin of Asbury United Methodist Church in Little Rock:

> *2-Year-Old Class Helper Needed.*

A strong child is preferred. He or she will be supervising unruly adults.

It was read in unison by the congregation of Prairie Grove United Methodist Church.
From the bulletin:

> *...I believe in the One who with love*
> *changed the hearts of the proud and with*
> *His life showed it is more important to*
> *serve than to be served....*
> *...I believe in peace, which is snot...*

So much for unison.

Michael D. Cummings, a member of the congregation, reports, "Our son Scott and a lady behind us, who shall not be named" —those two kept going— "but only by reading with great difficulty."

Nearly everybody else bowed out.

For Michael Cummings the moment was not lost.

"If this statement is correct about peace, then I could perhaps understand the motivation of the warring nations around the globe."

We have here four copies of the same bulletin from First United Methodist Church in Magnolia, on a day of visitation from the district superintendent. From the Order of Worship:

The Gloria Patri
The Words of Assurance
Moments of Personal Medication
The Prayer

Three bulletins arrived in the mail from anonymous senders. The fourth was signed by Dick Kirkpatrick.

"Although there have been a lot of flu and colds in Magnolia recently"—well, for everybody to dose up right there in church, come on!

But to get to Kirkpatrick's real beef.

"As a pharmacist, I only regret that I was not notified in advance, so that I could have set up a concession stand."

All of this reminded Ed Eason of something.

"We are charter members of the Woodland Heights Baptist Church in Conway. The church was formed about 15 months ago. In the early months we had no regular secretary, thus accepting typing help where we could get it."

One Sunday the bulletin carried these notations:

A.M. Service—Worship through tithes and
offerings.

P.M. Service—Worship of tithes and
offerings.

Ed Eason explains that this was not, as it might have appeared, a matter of Woodland Heights priorities. "Our problem was a lack of quality control."

She writes the warning from Conway. No matter what happens, don't even think of mentioning her name—"My pastor friend would kill me for sending this."
What she sends is a copy of the bulletin, mailed out by "Bro. John" with special enthusiasm because the Bethel church is observing the 90th anniversary of its founding.
And what a celebration, beginning with these lines from the bulletin:

Happy birthday to you!
Happy birthday to you!
Happy birthday,
Dead Bethel,
Happy birthday to you!

Sunday's bulletin is forwarded by a member of a church in southwest Little Rock:

SPECIAL MUSIC FOR SUNDAY—Sunday
morning we are to have a solo by Miss
[name deleted]. Sunday evening a quartet
is scheduled. Pray for the musicians.

One funny note and this congregation goes for the hook.

She was to be Sunday's pianist, so on Saturday afternoon Annette Greenland stopped by First Presbyterian Church in Stuttgart to pick up a copy of the bulletin.
The church secretary, Yvonne Shelton, was at home with a new baby.
Pulling substitute duty was Jan Davis, the church's former secretary.

Annette Greenland says, "The bulletin was hot off the press—er, copying machine—and Jan was typing her way through a stack of ministerial correspondence."

It was not easy.

"Bouncing around the office, trying to be patient and reasonably quiet, were Jan's twin sons, exuberant second-graders-to-be. This particular Sunday was the last one before the start of school.

The pianist left the church wondering how in the world Jan Davis was managing.

When she got home, Annette Greenland sat down and read in the bulletin, from the Prayer of Confession:

Forgive us our sins and erorrs.

Martha Bigley found the notice in her newspaper in Magnolia:

Seventh Day Adventists will show a film on what the Bible has to say about what happens to man when he dies at 7:30 p.m. at the VFW Hall.

It is more risk than Martha Bigley would take.

"If I were a man, I don't think I would go to this meeting."

Great Bible Puns

A reader without shame, L. Stell of Fordyce enters it in the Best Stressed Pun competition.

A painting contractor contracted to paint a church. He bought very cheap paint and thinned it very thin. The church looked good and the contractor was well-paid.

Two days later it rained. Most of the paint washed away. The pastor burst into the contractor's office, pointed his finger, and in his most hell-fire voice thundered, "Repaint, you thinner!"

Without question, the heat finally got to Ben Hicks at England.

Hicks has decided to share certain Bible facts.

"Did you know that the only major sport referred to in the Bible is baseball?"

Read from the top, as they say. "It starts out, in the big inning."

And doesn't stop there.

"The only automobile referred to in the Bible is the Honda. We know this after reading that the Disciples left in one Accord."

Everybody knows about the biblical reference to the land of opportunity—"Noah looked out from his Ark and Saw."

Ben Hicks notes with pride that no other state gets mentioned.

"The most important occupation in biblical days was firefighting. Even the Wise Men pursued this vocation. We know as much after reading that the Wise Men came from a far."

Having read—somewhere—the best jokes of 1926, Rev. William M. Wilder is inspired to identify the first businesswoman in the Bible.

Mr. Wilder is pastor of First United Methodist Church of Jonesboro.

Who was the first businesswoman in the Bible?

"Pharoah's daughter."

And how was Pharoah's daughter a businesswoman?

"She took a little prophet out of the bulrushes."

Mr. Wilder's congregation might want to take something out on somebody.

Pharoah's daughter had serious competition.

Hearing of William Wilder's report, another minister referred us to Proverbs.

This other minister asked not to be identified. We will respect his wishes, noting only that he is a man with newspaper connections, and an office right down the hall.

Proverbs 31:10: "Who can find a virtuous woman? For her price is far above rubies."

The minister says, "Of course, we'll never know what Ruby's price was."

Church Staff Job Descriptions

Reading how athletes are rated according to ability, Mark Short of Fayetteville dug out criteria for classifying members of a church staff:

Pastor—*Leaps tall buildings in a single bound, powerful as a switch engine, fast as a speeding bullet, walks on water if the sea is calm.*

Minister of Education—*Leaps short buildings with a running start, faster than a speeding BB, walks on water if he knows where the stumps are.*

Minister of Music—*Clears a Quonset hut, loses race with locomotive, can fire a speeding bullet, swims well.*

Church Secretary—*Lifts buildings to walk under them; kicks locomotives off the track; catches speeding bullets in her teeth; freezes water with a single glance; when God speaks, says, 'May I ask who's calling?'"*

With Sponsors Like These, How Can He Lose?

Displayed at the Seventh Day Adventist Church in Bentonville is a poster recommending the services of an operation called House Sitting, Inc.

Among the services offered are feeding fish, keeping dogs, picking up newspapers—all the things a family needs to feel good about while away from home.

The poster describes the owner of House Sitting, Inc., as a "Reliable, Honest, Christian Young Man."

To be precise, he is Michael Boothe, eleven.

And he has good backing.

"Supervised," the poster says, "by God and Mom."

(Re)Called by God

Getting Slicked in God's Service

The man who walked into the pastor's study wore one of those orange vests, the garb of a highway workman standing out on the landscape.

The vest afforded an official appearance. So did a piece of paper in the visitor's hand.

"Pastor, we're fixing a water line around the corner. Our boss man is away, and we badly need an emergency part that costs ten dollars and eighty cents."

The Rev. Andrew M. Hall glanced at the piece of paper. Written there was "$10.80."

The visitor continued in earnest, "If you'd let me have the money, I could get it back by the time church is over. When are you done—twelve o'clock?"

Andrew Hall only had a twenty dollar bill.

"Thank you very kindly, pastor," the vested one said, retreating through the study door. "Please pray that we'll get her finished."

If the preacher sent up any such words, they were deficient.

Andrew Hall has divided more than forty years of ministry between Arkansas and Florida.

The flock at First Baptist Church at Fayetteville can read this and sigh, "Well, they've ripped him off again down in Florida."

Serving as interim pastor at Fort Lauderdale, Mr. Hall is looking for an orange vest his own size.

He plans to "work my way" back to Fayetteville in April, in time to greet the doogwood and the redbud.

He had just assumed the pastorate of First Church at Fayetteville.

The man with hat in hand had one of those—call it a "crowbar indentation" on his scalp.

Andrew Hall tried not to stare. But not long before that, he had been slicked by a wheezing man down at Lake Wales, Florida.

In his Fayetteville study, the minister made a speech. He told his visitor about the many employment opportunities available around town.

Pain gathered in the man's face.

He stumbled around the desk, falling to his knees at the preacher's side.

The man with the crowbar indentation grasped Andrew Hall's hand and began praying for his attitude.

It was strong medicine. A prisoner in his own kingdom, Mr. Hall forked over cash.

The man came close to forgiving him.

Their car windows bore the joyous message "JUST MARRIED!" but there was no joy in the newlyweds' hearts, not when they chugged into Delray, Florida.

They had lost their honeymoon savings down at Key West. Poof! The money just disappeared.

Andrew Hall knew this one was for real.

He waved the painted car away from the church, feeling richly rewarded in this opportunity to serve. The grateful couple promised to return his money when they reached home in Tennessee.

Somewhere they turned left and headed south.

The police chief at Lake Wales almost laughed his badge off.

"There was this old man," Mr. Hall started explaining to the chief, a member of his church.

Older than dirt, the man was, and wheezing clouds of anguish.

When Mr. Hall opened his study door, the visitor signaled time to catch his breath. He poured some white "heart pills" into his hand and struggled to get them down.

"All he needed was a bus ticket to Tallahassee to pick up his pension check"—the police chief signaled time out, and completed the story—"and he would bring your money back Monday."

Yes, Andrew Hall will be heading home to Fayetteville as soon as he finds an orange vest.

The next man to slick him will have to get up mighty early.

Or might late.

Or somewhere in the middle.

Moved By The Spirit

A discussion here about amazing demonstrations of knowing the Bible reminded a Little Rock man about an amazing North Arkansas mountain preacher known as Brother Jamison.

Jamison might not have been Brother Jamison's real name. From a vantage point of sixty years removed, the Little Rock man speculates that the Brother part might have been subject to scrutiny also.

But Brother Jamison, at the time of World War I, commanded wide respect in Searcy County.

From his landlady, he commanded awe.

She introduced the Little Rock man, then a young mountain school teacher, to his amazing fellow roomer.

"Brother Jamison, tell again how you came to know the Bible."

Brother Jamison told again the amazing way the spirit had seized him.

"I had a trance. In the trance I laid back and the whites of my eyes rolled up. I don't know how long I stayed that way. When I sat up out of the trance, I could quote the Bible word for word."

The landlady's eyes rolled.

"John three sixteen," the young teacher said.

"How's that?" Brother Jamison said.

"John three sixteen."

Brother Jamison was not about to put up with a thing like that. He stomped out.

His vast knowledge of the Bible turned Brother Jamison into a man of great personal power.

"I am a man without fear," was the way he put it.

On a Saturday, the young teacher and Brother Jamison and two other men from the rooming house went exploring a cave in the mountains outside Leslie.

"It was a long drop, one hundred feet straight down, to get into the cave itself. We rigged a long rope around a tree and tied a crosspiece of wood, something to straddle, to the other end of the rope."

The young teacher descended first, lowered slowly by the men on the surface. Brother Jamison went second.

"I am a man without fear," he said, disappearing into the deepening twilight of the shaft. Halfway down, something happened and Brother Jamison started hollering.

"Lower me up! Lower me up!"

With the preacher hollering instructions, the three laymen managed to get him down and then back up out of the cave, after which Brother Jamison never took his fearlessness into the cave again.

In addition to knowing everything about the Bible and nothing about fear, Brother Jamison turned out to be an expert on geology.

Somewhere out in the mountains he discovered a giant lead mine.

Brother Jamison did not disclose his discovery to everybody. He let it be known, round-aboutly, to a member of his flock who was a merchant.

"Where is the mine?" the merchant asked.

Brother Jamison confided that he could let that part be known for the sum of $800.

The merchant went over to Marshall and drew $800 out of his bank and took it to Brother Jamison.

The location of the giant lead mine became a mystery. So did the location of Brother Jamison.

As fate had it, shortly after Brother Jamison got the $800 in his pocket, the spirit seized him again and commanded him to move on.

Caliber Used To Mean Something

It is good to see a resurgence in the want ads of the word "caliber." Business once again is on the lookout for persons who have it.

"CALIBER TYPE PERSON" the large type said this week. The position promised up to $18,000 to any person, a "decisional" person, whose caliber would fit him in.

It is high time. The word has been all but lost to recent generations.

There was a time when caliber was the most important thing a person had. No speaker from out of town ever got up without having his caliber pointed out. Certainly nobody ever got up to preach.

"This evening we are richly blessed to have with us a man of Brother Stoner's caliber."

In the cheerless sanctuary light, Brother Stoner's head was cast semidownward, his arms folded, one leg crossed over the other, his attention fixed on a cream-colored dress shoe, the toe of which was cast semiupward, a detached thing.

All eyes turned to look at Brother Stoner's caliber, which enlarged with the mention of it.

At age eight, and with feet that would not touch the floor, we guessed the revivalist's caliber to be about the same as the Swedish Angel's, the head approximately a 105 mm. howitzer shell, now grown quite still, fusing itself.

The regular preacher went on with the introduction. "And I know his message will be an inspiration to everyone."

Now Brother Stoner was unfolding, rising to his feet.

"What's a caliber?" We whispered this question to the man sitting on the pew beside us.

He leaned down and patted us on the knee, saying gently, "Shh," and then folded his own arms, as though to prepare for a confrontation.

"Is it over around Monticello?" This was asked as a last resort, the fact being that we figured "caliber" had to do with a tribe of large-headed people over in Drew County, where Brother Stoner had come to us from, a man of his caliber.

But then the place was deathly still, except for the word "Monticello," which hung in the air and turned our ears red, forcing us down in the pew.

The difference between Brother Stoner and Josip Bulletino was that Brother Stoner could blow himself up.

On the way home we got the answer. Our father's eyes were watering, but only from the time of day, and we knew he had survived the confrontation, just as he always had and always would.

He explained:

"Caliber is the diameter of a bore. Why did you ask?"

Identity Crisis At A Church Meeting

The Rev. Paul W. Sipes of Hot Springs got caught at a meeting in which factions went hammer and tongs over the question of "chairman" vs. "chairperson."

Mr. Sipes reports:

"Interestingly, there wasn't a soul present who was under sixty-five and very few under seventy, but the main argument for change was the argument of not appearing to be behind the times."

At least half the folks arguing for "chairperson" were men.

At least half of those arguing for "chairman" were women.

At least half of the time everybody seemed to be changing positions.

After forty-five minutes, the group agreed to dump the whole thing on its in-house retired minister, Paul Sipes.

"We'll leave it up to you," the chair(person)man said. "Which would you rather be called, Reverend Sipes, a chairman or a chairperson?"

The minister stood up, grabbing his coat and hat in the same movement, and declared, "I'd rather be called absent."

Which in five seconds he was.

Prayer and Preaching Both Work

The Rev. Andrew Hall of Fayetteville—and of Florida during cold weather—says it was told for the truth back when he was studying to be a preacher.

That was a while ago. But what is true remains true.

"There was this country preacher who prayed, "Lord, I thank thee that I am ignorant. Please keep me ignorant."

One deacon leaned over and whispered to another deacon, "The Lord answered that prayer before it was ever prayed."

We know just how that country preacher feels.

Josephine and Hoyt Dunlevy of Fort Smith have told us, "Things are never more confused than right after you have explained them."

We knew a great preacher who suffered the same way.

"Our preacher has to be the smartest man in the world," a good woman boasted over the fence to her next-door neighbor. "Nobody in the church can understand a word he says."

Four Discoveries and A Revelation on Sunday Morning

For his sermon topic last Sunday, the Rev. John Turner of Pulaski Heights Christian Church chose the joy of discovering God's power.

Which is not to say that there is joy in all of man's discoveries.

For example, when John Turner arrived at the church Sunday morning, he discovered that he had left his sermon at home.

There was still plenty of time.

Mr. Turner made the return drive home, about two miles. He found his sermon on the breakfast table and there made a second discovery.

The message was soaking wet. John and Judy Turner's eighteen-month-old daughter, Carissa, earlier had done her breakfast number there.

"I remembered seeing her playing at the table. She had turned a glass of water over my sermon."

By shaking and wiping, the minister managed to save his words for the morning.

"They were somewhat blurred," he recalled.

But Mr. Turner left the house in good shape for the work ahead.

Which was when he made his third discovery of the morning.

"I guess it was just as I closed the door, locked it, that I realized I'd left the keys inside."

Car key and door key.

The joy of discovering how to get into a locked house when it's time to be getting to church is not a joy unrestrained.

The minister, in fact, could not get back into his house.

Except for one long-shot possibility.

The Turners have a dog, Rowsby Woof. Down at the bottom of the back door, Rowsby Woof has her own door, hinged access to the backyard and a way back inside.

The minister of Pulaski Heights Christian Church went around back, got down on his knees and surveyed the situation. It was not promising.

As the church secretary, Sheila Bowman, would put it later, "No, his size would not help him get through a dog's door."

Mr. Turner took off his coat.

Then he took off his vest.

He got down and began to squirm into Rowsby Woof's door.

At this points it depends on which member of the congregation you are talking to.

Some say their minister backed through the dog's door feet first.

Other say, no, it was the other way. Still others say the preacher employed several versions of both, more or less coming and going at the same time. It is difficult to get the accounts straight because all of the tellers are laughing their heads off—in a respectful manner, of course.

The minister's personal accounting to us suggested a conventional head-first entry—"Rowsby was licking my face practically the whole time."

That was more Sunday morning fun than Rowsby had come to expect.

Now John Turner made his largest discovery of the morning.

"I was stuck in the door. I just got to a place where I couldn't go any farther, and I couldn't back out, either."

Never mind the success of the project.

"I accomplished what I set out to do. Once I got far enough inside, I was able to reach up and open the door. But that didn't help me."

When a man is part of a door, it doesn't much matter whether he is opened or closed.

Mr. Turner struggled, and he longed for the power of discovery.

Did he hear angel voices?

"I began to have images. What would be happening at the church?"

Would they come and find him slightly ajar?

Something inspired John Turner to free himself. How long it took he cannot say. Probably not the eternity that went by.

"I just worked at it until I got out. Maybe I wasn't stuck much more than five minutes."

He hurried to the church with his blurred sermon, arriving with just a minute to spare.

Unfortunately, during that minute he explained to somebody what had happened. The account was passed on to somebody else, and then to still a third member of the congregation.

When pulpit time came, there was nothing to do but get up there and tell the whole thing.

The Pastor Trap

The Rev. Paul Sipes is preparing a note of sympathy for the Rev. John Turner, who at church time on Sunday morning got stuck in a ground-level dog's door, trying to get into, or out of, his locked-up house.

Paul Sipes is retired and living in Hot Springs.

"Many good people will not forget the morning that services in our church in Kansas proceeded without their minister, me, although I was trying as hard as John Turner to be with them."

Mr. Sipes was trapped in a small room that adjoined his church office.

"I began kicking on the door, knowing full well the racket would resound to the back of the sanctuary and probably frighten the congregation half out of its collective wits."

When the kicking started, the organist played louder. And faster.

A voice came from beyond the door where the minister was trapped "Who's in there?"

Paul Sipes identified himself.

"Oh, yes, Brother Sipes." The doorknob was tugged several times. The voice said, "You stay right where you are, Brother Sipes" then went away.

It took three ushers ten more minutes to liberate their preacher.

Word had preceded him to the pulpit. Mr. Sipes arrived in a crescendo of organ music and looked into a sea of contorted faces.

He told the congregation, "Since we're running late, I'll dispense with the announcements except to say that the building committee will meet immediately after services to discuss installing a new lock on the pastor's washroom door."

What was left of services went about as reverently as you would expect.

Sympathy for the Mowed-Over

Nobody will be more philosophical about seeing the growing season end than John Gipson.

Philosophical as in overjoyed.

Growing season as in grass growing season.

Yard grass.

Joh Gipson is a minister. Sixth and Izard Church of Christ in Little Rock.

As such, he knows there is a time to reap and a time to sow.

A time to water and a time to mow.

A time to sprawl backward and get half-drowned in the kiddie swimming pool.

"It's about fifteen feet across." Mr. Gipson described the pool to his congregation. On Sunday morning, he was dried out and no longer looking like a prune.

With a garden hose, the pool requires forty days and forty nights to get it up to eighteen inches of water. That is the level ordered by Mr. Gipson's grandchildren, Kate and Patrick.

They were not present when Granddad performed his backward one-and-a-half.

"I pulled the mower in on top of me."

The blade cut off the heel of one shoe.

When his head got underwater, that's when John Gipson turned the mower loose.

"I could have mowed myself to death."

Some will wonder, now what did that have to do with preaching the gospel?

Shame on those doubting Thomases.

In the pulpit, Preacher Gipson had reached that point at which Peter and John showed profound sympathy to a lame man at the temple gate.

Not sympathy with alms, for they had none. But the sympathy of Christian caring.

"But not everybody has an eye for sympathy," John Gipson told his flock.

When he staggered to the house, soaking wet, half a shoe and all his dignity gone, his wife Beth opened the door and observed, "That would have made a good home video."

'Clipping' in the Pulpit, Not Just on the Field

Our man John Workman was the visiting preacher Sunday at St. Paul's United Methodist Church.

The subject of his sermon was "The People of God in Transit."

As Dr. Workman reached the pulpit, he noticed a piece of paper, a clipping, left there by somebody. He gave the paper no attention.

Or he tried not to.

"It kept getting tangled up in my notes," he said. "I had to keep setting it aside."

Finally the piece of paper would not be ignored. Just before announcing the final hymn, Dr. Workman looked directly at the clipping.

He shared what he saw with the St. Paul's congregation.

"I'm looking here at a cartoon in which there is a preacher wearing a robe not unlike the one I'm wearing. He is bald, wearing glasses and portly, not unlike the preacher you are looking at."

Dr. Workman told the congregation that hidden behind the cartoon preacher's pulpit was a television set broadcasting the reminder, "Super Bowl Sunday."

The people of God were anxious to be in transit, all right.

The visiting minister told somebody later, "They did everything but give me a two-minute warning."

Wave Those Hankies, Sisters

The Rev. Samuel Adkins decided "Rowdy Rags" were a good idea, so at First Baptist Church of Sheridan he led off his Sunday sermon with such a proposal.

A word of explanation:

Supporters of the basketball team at the University of Arkansas at Little Rock wave "Rowdy Rags" to give the Trojan players a lift.

This newspaper's religion editor, John S. Workman, said why not the same for preachers?

Hand out "Rowdy Rags" to worshippers entering the sanctuary. When the minister begins scoring points, if he does, let the congregation join in, waving and shouting, "Go, Rev, go!"

At Sheridan, Sam Adkins was reading John Workman's proposal to his congregation. Even as the words came out, he caught in the corner of his eye the movement of a white handkerchief in the choir.

"You see," the minister said, gesturing toward the faithful sister in the alto section. "Our choir already is getting in the spirit."

With those words hanging in the air, a response came from the bass section, the voice of the man married to the woman waving her hanky.

"Don't get excited, preacher. She's just having another one of those hot flashes."

Let Him Among You Who Is Left-Handed Cast The First Stone

Arthur Terry is a retired minister living in Magnolia.

"I am eighty-five and a half. My steps have gotten much shorter and my tales much longer. I think I still have all my marbles, but they do tend to roll around a bit."

The latest tale Arthur Terry refers to is about the Rev. Jim Keith of First Methodist Church in Magnolia.

"Our senior minister is loved by the membership and the community because they are sure he loves them. But he has a subtle way of coming down hard on the congregation."

Jim Keith made a confession from his pulpit.

"I am left-handed." He let the disclosure set in. "I was born left-handed."

Pastor Keith paused, then made a really dramatic revelation.

"Everybody is born left-handed. They stay that way until they sin."

He Cannot Tell A Lie

The Rev. Larry Powell of Lonoke was telling friends about the plight of a minister who lived some years ago near Prescott.

This preacher had a garden, along with some chickens and pigs, as did most of the families in his flock.

One of those families, good-hearted as it was, did not get down and pray over neatness. Their chickens and pigs were welcome anywhere on the place. It was widely understood that the livestock spent considerable time in the house.

The lady of that family came by the preacher's house one day with a big frosted cake.

He thanked her profusely. As soon as she was gone, the preacher said a prayer and threw the cake over the fence to his pigs.

Next day they met at the general store.

"Preacher, how did you like the cake?" the good woman asked proudly.

The Rev. Larry Powell says this preacher wouldn't lie with a gun pointed at his head.

He said to the woman, "Let me tell you something! A cake like that doesn't last long at our house."

Through the Eyes of His Heart

Our sporting colleague, Jim Bailey, is not certain how this can be told, only that it should be.

So he tells it just right.

At Texarkana, to close out his weekly church service at a nursing home, the minister pulled out a harmonica and played a hymn.

This did not thrill the minister's wife. It did, however, bring particular joy to one resident of the home. About ninety, she had wheeled down the hall for the service, the oldest person able to make it.

From a sack of possessions on her lap, the woman took out a harmonica of her own. As the minister finished his hymn, she said, "Let's play a duet."

They played a harmonica duet.

Jim Bailey is not sure about the song. From a critic's standpoint it could have been "Shall We Gather at the River," or it could have been "I Dropped My Dolly in the Dirt."

But play they did.

These duets became a regular thing, closing the nursing home worship service for the next several weeks.

Then the minister's wife confiscated his harmonica.

He did not object. In truth, he was relieved. But how could one say that to a hymn-playing partner, four score and ten?

"I don't have my harmonica today," he said at the close of the next service.

The oldest woman smiled. With her harmonica already in hand, she dug through her bag of possessions, and from somewhere in there pulled out another harmonica.

"That's all right," she said. "I have another one."

This good woman is known throughout the nursing home as being partial to snuff. Not merely a pinch here and there. She is regarded as one of the great dippers of all time.

Nor was the minister unaware of it.

If he gulped, only the minister knew it. He accepted the harmonica, not quite looking at it, looking instead at those faces arrayed before him.

Then he looked at his smiling partner.

Paul says in Ephesians 1:18: "I pray also that the eyes of your heart may be enlightened, in order that you may know the hope to which He has called you..."

Through the eyes of his heart, the minister saw no snuff.

The two played the service to a close.

At the door, several clapped him on the back.

"Brother Bob," somebody said warmly, "you're a lot bigger man than when you came in."

A Wrong Turn
At The West Fork

The Rev. Bob Vaughn left the promised land of Northwest Arkansas to go preach to sinners down in Texas.

Apparently there is no end to the work to be done.

But at a reunion recently at Ridgeview Baptist Church in Fayetteville, Bob Vaughn had to get something off his chest.

It was a confession.

The Rev. Andrew Hall of Fayetteville has been thoughtful enough to gather up the details and share them.

It is for Mr. Vaughn's benefit.

The more persons who get in on a confession, the better off the guilty party becomes.

Especially if the guilty party is someone else.

It was twelve years ago. Or maybe fifteen.

"The late Rev. Dove of Fayetteville knew young Bob Vaughn before Bob left for the seminary."

Those years in earnest study were completed.

"Bob finished his training and came out aching to find himself a church of his own."

The Vaughns were visiting relatives in Fayetteville.

Mrs. Vaughn answered the telephone.

"Yes, Brother Dove, I'm sure Bob will be happy to supply the pulpit at West Fork Sunday."

She turned and conveyed the good news to her husband.

The Rev. Bob Vaughn was ecstatic.

You might even say light-headed.

"On Sunday morning, he sailed right on through West Fork, where the people were waiting for him, and some miles later pulled up in front of the First Baptist Church of Winslow."

Now get this.

"It just so happened that Winslow, too, was pastorless."

The church's leadership convened.

"Nobody was quite sure who had invited Vaughn to preach, but one deacon's business is everybody's puzzle. Bob preached his sugarstick sermon."

Andrew Hall explains that "sugarstick" is preacher talk for giving them the sweetest you've got.

It was as though this young preacher had dropped out of the Ozark heavens.

"The saints of Winslow conferred. Yes, Brother Vaughn would be able to return for the evening services."

Which he did. Brother Bob Vaughn drove back through West Fork, going and coming, his wheels barely touching the blacktop. Not from speed. From a soaring spirit.

"Following evening service, a business meeting was held. Brother Vaughn was extended a call as pastor. He was delighted."

It was Monday morning. Brother Vaughn answered the telephone.

"Why, yes, Brother Dove. How are you?"

Niceties were exchanged.

Then Brother Dove inquired in that wonderfully warm tone of his, "How did the sermon go at West Fork?"

West Fork!

Brother Vaughn steered his mentor gently. "Er, ah, Brother Dove. You mean Winslow, don't you?"

Right then it all came down.

"To this day, he confessed at the Ridgeview Church reunion, Vaughn has no earthly idea why he went to Winslow instead of West Fork."

The young preacher and the Winslow congregation came together warmly.

"He stayed there five years as their pastor."

Before going away to work with Texas sinners, Bob Vaughn returned to Fayetteville to preach in town.

"He served at Ridgeview," says Andrew Hall, who then adds with admiration, "Without driving on through to Elkins."

The people of West Fork?

"They couldn't understand why Brother Dove would promise to send them a preacher."

Not a man of Brother Dove's stature.

"And then nobody ever showed up."

Expectations Not Revealed

Pauline Hammons doesn't identify the associate pastor, only provides his title.

"He is especially gifted at lifting our spirits, making us feel glad we have come into the Lord's house of worship."

This Sunday he bounded to the front with his usual energy.

"I came expecting this morning! How many of you came expecting?"

The response was virtual silence.

The associate pastor cranked it up a bit, waving his arm to include the entire congregation.

"I said I came expecting this morning! How many of you came expecting?"

Pauline Hammons says that many church ladies ducked their heads, and widespread twittering was not well suppressed.

The associate pastor turned to the choir, "I came expecting! Did you come expecting?"

Finally the challenge.

"I challenge you! Every one of you come back tonight expecting!"

Mrs. Hammons has no statistics about the evening service.

Out of the
Mouths of Babes

A Flood of Devotion

Mr. and Mrs. Paul Rice are getting their religious education enriched at nightly devotional sessions with their three children, aged seven years down to fourteen months.

Mr. Rice is a Missionary Baptist minister at North Little Rock. Mrs. Linda Rice keeps progress reports on their family devotionals.

Progress, more or less.

"Why did God send the flood in Noah's day?"

That question at a recent devotional was answered by seven-year-old Danny Rice as though any dummy would know it, "So the boat would float."

Mrs. Rice reports that "we also have a clearer understanding of forgiveness of sins now."

Asked what good things God did when He was obeyed, Danny Rice explained, "He gives your sins away."

The minister's wife has no idea who has been getting her sins.

"I hope I never meet her."

Her son's knowledge extends beyond religion and into medicine. Mr. Rice is facing surgery for gallstones, by which is meant, as Danny explains to visitors, making a circle the size of a grapefruit with his hands:

"My Dad's going to have his gallbrain cut out because he's got a rock that big."

Mrs. Rice concludes:

"I used to pray for patience, but the Lord kept answering me with another child. Now I just thank Him for the little patience I have left."

Out Of The Mouths Of Babes

At the beginning of the children's sermon, the Rev. Tony Holifield produced a glass of tea and asked the youngsters of First United Methodist Church in Heber Springs, "Boys and girls, does anybody know what this is?"

A small child of unfortunate parents volunteered in a loud speculative voice, "Beer?"

The Rev. Jim Farmer can sympathize.

At Park Hill Christian Church last week, Jim Farmer used spray cans to demonstrate the point of his sermonette for young folks.

The point was that spray cans had many different and useful functions to perform painting, shampooing rugs, freshening rooms.

It was the same with individuals, the minister told the little ones assembled for their special message. What kinds of persons will we be?

"What would we get," Mr. Farmer asked, "if we put this can down on top of your head and pushed the button?"

"Blood," a small voice replied.

So Much To Be Thankful For

Thanksgiving Day has come and gone. But it is never too late to be thankful.

What more eloquent reminder than that from the six-year-old girl in Sarah Parton's Sunday school class in Hot Springs?

The child bowed her head and said, "Lord, there's so damn much to be thankful for I don't know where to begin."

Our own son, Bern, when he was small, knew where to begin.

With bowed head on Thanksgiving Day, he spoke from a grateful heart, "I'm so thankful there isn't no gorilla in the carport storage room."

Weren't we all!

At Pine Bluff, Trudy Foster was discussing with her Sunday school children how people tend to forget the Lord's role in their lives.

"We just go on accepting his many good things, as if we were entitled to them."

The six-year-olds thought of things they wouldn't have without help from the Lord.

"Your parrots," one said.

All the children agreed. You could not just walk down the street and pick out some parrots.

"Something to eat," said another class member.

Oh, absolutely!

If God didn't give us something to eat, there wouldn't be half as much food. The children agreed that all you'd get to eat at McDonald's would be liver and french fries.

Trudy Foster said to a youngster who sat pensively taking things in, "How about you, Lloyd?"

Lloyd said, "Your mother and father."

Mrs. Foster nodded. Yes, parrots already had been covered.

Lloyd said, "Something to eat."

Lloyd obviously was a good listener.

"All right," he said finally, "I'll tell you what."

And he did.

"I'm glad about God because He lets us get out of Hallowe'en alive."

The word for the day was "gratitude." As Sunday school class in Fort Smith drew to a close, Bernice Brown challenged her youngsters.

"All right. Let's go around the room. Each of you tell in one word what you have gratitude to the Lord for."

Things went smoothly until David.

David is eight. "My gratitude is not having to go to Sunday school but once a week."

David is Bernice Brown's nephew.

The teacher kept cool. She said, "That's more than one word, David."

David said he knew.

"But if I say the real word about Sunday school, you'll run tell Mama."

Margaret Tilley of Harrison recalls a Sunday school class of twelve-year-olds taught by her son Ab.

"Ab had to miss one week, so he asked his substitute to fill in."

Faye Dixon was the substitute. She graciously agreed.

Ab's mother goes on, "Faye was patting herself on the back, feeling assured she had matched Ab's rapport with the group."

Faye dismissed the class by having each child give a short prayer.

One bowed his head and asked earnestly, "Please God, let Ab be back next Sunday."

First grader Ryan Manley was sick of the weather.

Not in modern times, meaning not in at least three or four days, had Ryan seen anything but rain and mist and fog and clouds.

Fed up was what he was.

Then, as Ryan and his mother were leaving school at Jacksonville, the sun broke through.

You don't take that for granted.

The youngster declared to the ceiling of the car, "Nice goin', God!"

A Child's Prayer

We have been instructed, under penalty of murder, or worse, to report no names or addresses in the unfolding of a human drama in a town located, let us say, across the river from Little Rock.

What unfolded is described by a friend of the family.

It occurred some weeks ago, but the reverberations are still out there reverberating.

An eight-year-old boy who attends a church school was obliged to stand, along with each of his classmates, and report his New Year's resolutions.

In a situation like that, you have to come up with something.

The family friend relates:

"This youngster stood up and said he had been praying that his dad would quit drinking."

Properly moved, the entire class took up the prayer.

The truth is that the father who got prayed for owns one Coors beer, a can that has been in the refrigerator for going on seven months.

Word of the mass praying reached home. All those little hands folded, heads earnestly bowed.

According to the family friend, the eight-year-old boy has acquired something he can really pray for.

"He's praying he makes it to nine."

And They All Turned Thanks Together

In Monticello, after the Sunday guests were gone, Mrs. Ray Pearcy heard her young grandson grumbling about the visiting preacher's dinner table prayer.

Jamie Pearcy, eight, said, "You couldn't hear half of what he said."

That wasn't all.

"And the other half you couldn't understand what he meant."

That wasn't all, either.

"And the part you could hear and understand, there's no way you could make yourself do it."

A North Little Rock woman says a youngster she knows stopped everybody from eating because his grandfather hadn't yet come to the table.

"We can't eat until Papaw comes and reads the plate."

The Rev. Ross Williams is pastor of Lake Ouachita Baptist Church.

He has a granddaughter, Christy Williams, four, who said the table blessing the other day.

"Amen" wasn't the end of it.

Before anybody could look up, the child added, "And don't you forget it!"

His own flock should be aware that Mr. Williams has been trying to say the same thing all along.

Jim Stockton of Harrison is proud of the way his son, Jamie, four, is learning prayers at St. John's Day School.

It enables the youngster to provide spiritual leadership at the family dinner table.

"All heads were bowed," Jim Stockton reports, "after Jamie volunteered to lead us in the pre-meal prayer 'God is Good.'"

Unfortunately, Jamie forgot "God is Good."

All heads got re-bowed as he decided to lead in the prayer, "Hands Folded."

Jamie forgot that one, too.

He looked up at the family with more than a little exasperation.

"Can we just pledge the flag instead?"

Which the Stocktons did.

Jim Stockton notes, "This may be a new trend for American family meals in keeping with the rebirth of patriotism in this country."

Mack Stanley reports on a trip a friend of his made from Oklahoma City to Spiro.

Traveling with the man was his grandson, a youngster of five.

They stopped for lunch at Okemah.

When the food was brought, the man started digging in.

The youngster stopped him.

"Wait for me to turn thanks, Grandpa!"

This came out in such a loud voice, everybody in the dining room stopped eating.

Mack Stanley says, "It seemed to the man that every head turned in his direction. He was embarrassed."

The youngster instructed further, "Everybody ought to turn thanks, Grandpa."

While the boy prayed out loud, the redfaced granddad stole a quick look around to see how many diners were enjoying his discomfort.

Every head in the place was bowed.

They Don't Make Hymns Like They Used To

Tooby Wood of Greers Ferry was scandalized when her four-year-old grandson asked, "What's a bosom fly?"

She complained to Granddad Harry Wood, "That's what we get for letting them live in that neighborhood. There's no telling what all he's learning."

Grandma declared to the youngster, "I've never heard of one of what you just said." Some things cannot be uttered.

Her grandson said, "Oh, yes, you have, Tooby. Every Sunday the preacher sings it."

You can't imagine how proud it makes Harry and Tooby, that their little one would go around with his head filled with religious music:

"Jesus, lover of my soul, let me to Thy bosom fly."

It must be the neighborhood.

Or it may be a stage common in all children. Ask Cathy Williams of Fort Smith.

One Sunday the service at Central Presbyterian Church had been particularly inspiring.

As Cathy Williams and her daughter drove home, they sang some songs.

Nearly there, nine-year-old Emily sang at the top of her voice, "Praise God from Whom all blessings flow. Praise him, you preachers down below."

Cathy Williams is certain that her daughter's tribute had nothing to do with anybody preaching at Central Presbyterian.

Sid Johnson admits that learning to read can rob life of some of its real joys.

It robbed him and his sister of singing at the clothes-line.

"While 'Bringing in the Sheaves' and 'Bringing in the Sheets' may have connected, we failed to appreciate it at that early age. Alas."

According to Ward Turley, his brother sang it a different way.

"My brother used to sing an old song called 'Bringing in the Shes.' He was quite a ladies' man and, as I recall, very adept at the task."

Ralph W. Davis remembers as a child going home from the Baptist church at Stephens with a new and joyful song in his heart.

Who is on the Lord's side, who will make reply?
Who is on the Lord's side, Master here am I.

Only that was not quite how young Ralph heard it. He came into the house singing...

Who is on the Lord's side, who will make a pie?
I am on the Lord's side, mash 'em in the eye.

Noah Morris, age six, of Little Rock, has his parents thinking seriously.

The youngster goes around singing a song he wrote.

"Reluctant God, if I met Jesus, what would I do to entertain Him?"

Noah's dad, Dan Morris, says the grownups are stumped.

"What is this? Is it Baptist? New Wave Gospel?"

The Christmas Story, by Josh

Josh Potts, age eight, is the son of John and Donna Potts, who live on the west end of Crow Mountain near Russellville.

Josh goes to school at Atkins, second grade. His mother is a teacher there.

There is a bunch of family history.

For example, Josh's grandfather, George Potts, is the postmaster at Pottsville. It was Kirkbride Potts, Josh's great-great-great-grandfather, who built Potts Tavern, on the Butterfield Stage route, and wound up getting the town of Pottsville named for him.

But that is not the story here.

The story here is Christmas.

Josh Potts has written out the story.

"A woman called Merre is a special woman. But she doesn't know it yet. She was a good woman. She didn't know that she is going to have a baby. And she doesn't know he is going to be a great king."

Merre got up feeling poorly.

"One morning she didn't feel well so she went to the doctor. The doctor said she was going to have a baby. So she got ready. But she thought for awhile and she said I have to get married if I am going to have a baby. She saw a man who was just right."

The ideal husband and father.

"He was single and lonely and he loved kids. So she thought of something. She would run into him and then she would ask to go out on a date. So she did and he said yes and so they went on a date. They fell in love and he asked her if she would marry him and she said yes."

The man's name? He was Joseph.

Merre forgot to tell him something.

"So Merre and Joseph got married. On their honeymoon a friend invited them to a party just for them. A lot of people were there. First they ate and then they danced and danced until Merre's stomach began to hurt."

That's when Merre remembered, on their honeymoon, to tell Joseph something.

"She said I forgot to tell you I am pregnant.

"Joseph smiled and said we need to get you somewhere you can have the baby at."

In those days, you could not just call a cab and head out for the hospital.

"A friend said I know where she can stay but it is not much. Anyway there is a barn close by where you can stay. And if he doesn't let you in tell them I said to let you in."

Of course, Josh Potts does not claim to have been there.

How could he have been, an eight-year-old? And that so very long ago.

But the events of that night are clear to Josh, as you shall see.

"And that night she had a baby. A star was above the barn. The baby lay in the hay. That night angels sang all night. And the star shone for a long time."

Such a star!

"Three wise men followed the star but they did not get there until he was four years old. They brought treasure. And then he was king forever."

We asked George Potts, the Pottsville postmaster, how this assignment had come to his grandson.

Granddad said this was not an assignment.

"I think Josh just wrote it on his own."

Josh Potts concluded his story:

"And that's how Christmas is a birthday party. A birthday party for a King. Merry Christmas."

Dogs In The Manger,
No Yell, No Yell

Because they handed out the Nativity Scene acting roles early, there still is time to work through the confusion.

John Woodruff got the report from some big people at church.

One of the children came home declaring proudly, "I'm going to play a dog."

It didn't sound right. Oxen, his folks had heard of. And asses. And sheep.

But nobody could remember a Nativity Scene play with a dog in the manger.

The child insisted there was no mistake.

"I'm going to play a shepherd."

Hannah Clark came home from kindergarten with the report that she and her schoolmates were having a good time singing Christmas songs.

"But why do we have to sing them so quiet?"

Her mother didn't understand.

"What do you mean, sing quiet?" Nancy Clark said.

Hannah explained, "Well, the very first song we sang was 'No Yell, No Yell.'"

That's the old favorite that ends, "Born is the king of Israyell."

For us it is never Christmas without recalling that child's version of "Silent Night," sung here so many years ago that by now the child must be grown up.

When sung with great feeling, it remains as sitrring as ever:

Round John Virgin, mother and child,
Holy infant so limber and wild,

Sleep is heavenly plee-EASE,
SLEE-eep is heavenly please.

Mrs. Roger Meador of Conway recalls that her son, Mark, never got that close. Mark sang it, "Drown one virgin."

He was the same soloist who stood before his kindergarten class and sang, instead of "the cattle are lowing," "the cattle are loaded."

Linda and Phil Lamb and their young son, Sparky, were leaving church at Trinity Presbyterian when the preacher called out to them.

"All right, now, you all have a merry Christmas!"

Sparky Lamb is not quite four.

He called back, "Humbug!"

Phil Lamb was as surprised as he was scandalized by what his son did.

"I've never said humbug in my life," Lamb insisted. "Neither has Linda."

Children naturally know certain things.

At First United Methodist Church of Searcy, the Rev. William D. Elliott wanted to make a point about the singing of angels.

As he addressed the children at their special time in the church service, Mr. Elliott asked, "Who provided the music the night Jesus was born?"

A hand shot up, and a small voice said everybody knew the answer to that.

"It was the little drummer boy."

Joseph and the Wise(acre) Men

Dr. V.O. McNabb of Morrilton is not at liberty to identify the church.

"The kids were allowed and encouraged to write their own script. The play was performed at the pre-Christmas candlelight service.

Thus, young Joseph and young Mary approached the young innkeeper and inquired about a room.

The keeper explained that there was no room at the inn.

Young Joseph, raising his voice: "My wife is pregnant and expecting a baby any day. We must have a room!"

Young Innkeeper: "I'm sorry, but that is not my fault. I had nothing to do with that."

Young Joseph: "Me neither."

Speaking of Christmas Eve, it has been done before, but never with more finesse.

At Concord United Methodist Church in Lonoke County, the Wise Men were rehearsing their part of the Nativity story.

Larry Powell got the details from somebody.

"Ah, yes. The Wise Men."

In costume, three young Concord men practiced their approach to the manger.

"They were concentrating hard on trying to appear smitten with adoration."

A solemn moment.

When, lo! One of the visitors from the East reached inside his robe and pulled out a fire extinguisher.

Solemnly, he announced, "We have come from a far."

A Gift for the Baby Jesus

We are indebted to John Malone for his outstanding report on how things went this year in the live manger scene at Pocahontas Methodist Church.

The role of Baby Jesus was performed by the now distinguished actor, Tom Riffel, age six months.

Patty and Kirby Riffel, parents of the star, sat enthralled in the congregation.

John Malone reports, "The Baby Jesus made it through the first half of the program in great shape. Then he became a little restless."

In the live manger scene, Mary was played by teen-ager Robyn Harris. When Baby Jesus began howling, Mary did what any young mother would do. She handed off to Joseph.

Joseph was, in fact, teen-ager Chad Couch. You don't get to be Joseph by being a dummy. Joseph handed Baby Jesus off to the nearest angel, in real life teen-ager Dawn Gutteridge.

Baby Jesus went around the manger like a hot potato.

Talk about a live scene!

John Malone says of the sound effects, "It was a pretty even battle between the crying baby and the twenty little singers in the choir."

Here came the wise men.

"The gold, frankincense and myrrh were coming down the aisle."

Malone saw that one of the wise men walked a little ahead of the others, moving with the urgency of a greater wisdom.

"He went straight to Joseph."

And to all those of Pocahontas Methodist Church, what was the greatest gift of all?

It wasn't the gold. It wasn't the frankincense. It wasn't the myrrh.

It was the pacifier.

Taking His Name In Vain,
For Gosh Sakes!

She readily takes the rap for it, Peggy Treiber of Fayetteville:

"As an adult, I acquired the unfortunate habit of using the Lord's name in vain in situations I find particularly stressful, such as when the washing machine overflows and soaks the wall-to-wall carpeting."

This would not do.

"In the interest of self-improvement I decided to break the habit, but did not become sufficiently motivated until my then two-year-old son achieved overnight the ability to parrot anything, including the vainly used Lord's name."

At age two, Adrian got it down pat.

Peggy Treiber relates, "Rather than panicking, I chose to correct him calmly and without undue emphasis."

This was so the child would not discover what kind of power he might have, especially in public.

"Each time Adrian became angry because the cat would not permit itself to be tied to the banister, or because his toothbrush could not be forced through the grate of the bathroom wall heater, I gently reminded him that he should change his phrase to 'For gosh sakes!' He always obliged."

The years flew by, or one and a half years did.

Peggy Treiber was driving Adrian, now three-and-a-half, to school last week. He noted that certain of the trees stayed green all the time. What made those trees so special?

Mom replied, as they say, in a richly meaningful way, "Because that's the way God made them."

Her son corrected her, "You mean Gosh, Mom. Gosh made the trees."

There is a Mother's Day card that says, "Motherhood is so rewarding."

Peggy Treiber is feeling so rewarded.

So is Marilyn Johnson.

Dr. Andrew M. Hall says Marilyn Johnson, "her distinguished mayor-ness" of Fayetteville, told it on herself.

Her seven-year-old son, John David, attended First Baptist Sunday school the day the lesson was on Jesus' healing of Simon Peter's mother-in-law.

Winding up the lesson, the teacher put things into a practical frame of reference.

"Tell me, children, how could one be raised from the dead nowadays?"

That was no problem for John David.

"At my house, my mom would do it."

Theology Revisited

James Ponder, age eighty-three, assists with activities at Fayetteville's First Baptist Church.

It is Mr. Ponder who shares some very good news.

Four youngsters, eight-year-old boys, were having a heavy theological discussion on the steps of a farmhouse near Dutch Mills, southwest of Fayetteville.

The subject was the End of Time.

James Ponder notes, "They didn't realize adult ears were picking up on the spirited discussion."

One boy painted a grim picture of the Last Days. Lightning. Falling stones. The whole works.

But a pal put it in perspective.

"No sweat," he said. "When the Lord comes, us cool ones will go right on to heaven."

It was in Hot Springs that the Rev. Larry D. Powell conducted a confirmation class, five youths, ages twelve and thirteen, who had an eye toward Palm Sunday, when they would be received into full membership of the church at Oaklawn United Methodist.

The pastor strained meticulously at the origins and meanings of baptism, Holy Communion, and various prominent matters of belief.

After three weeks of study and interchange, the work was completed. Mr. Powell confidently raised a wrap-up question:

"Now, then, when did the church begin?"

Brows furrowed.

A youth asked, "Do you mean *this* particular building?"

The minister said, "No, *the* church as an institution. When was the *first church* founded?"

The youths pondered back through the ages, calling on what they had learned, deducing logically.

"Hmmmm," sighed one, lost in profound intellectual exploration. "Gosh. That probably goes back at least to the Little House on the Prairie."

As a theological authority, that youngster ranks right up there with one who told her Sunday school teacher that her favorite Bible character was Solomon.

The teacher was immensely pleased.

"Why Solomon," she asked.

The youngster beamed and said, "Because he was so kind to ladies and animals."

The teacher's mood changed, but she had to know more. "Who told you that?"

The student said, "Nobody. It says right here in the Bible, 'Solomon kept seven hundred wives and three hundred porcupines.'"

Dr. Robert B. Moore has stopped wondering whether his grandchildren are getting proper spiritual treatment

Dr. Moore is a minister.

Little Rob was in a hospital in West Virginia.

"As I got to Rob's room, the surgeon was just leaving. He had showed Rob the stitches and explained how he removed a cyst from Rob's lower right rib."

It turned out that Rob's Bible studies begin at the same place as Granddad's. In the Garden of Eden.

The youngster looked at his scar, profoundly puzzled.

"Does this mean I'm going to have a wife?"

Myrle Ringland tells about a youngster's first visit to a new Sunday school class.

Myrle lives in Mena. She is not naming the church.

"When he got home, the boy's mother asked what the lesson was about."

The youngster was hesitant.

"Well, there was a man named Moses whose people were being mistreated by some bad people. God told Moses to lead his people to another land."

So they all set out, thousands of them.

"After awhile, they came to this big river. Or it might have been a ocean."

The boy paused. Then he went on, "Moses called the Corps of Engineers and they built pontoon bridges. After all his people had made it over, the bridges were taken down and the bad people drowned when they tried to get across."

The boy's mother was amazed. "Is that what they taught you?"

The boy said, "Mother, you wouldn't believe what they taught us."

God's Umbrella

All his life, which is nine years, Jamie Patterson has wanted to be a preacher.

The youngster was telling his grandfather, J.D. Patterson of Fort Smith, what his first sermon was going to be about.

"It's God's umbrella."

The elder Patterson asked for details.

Jamie said, "That's all there is to it. God has this big umbrella and everybody is protected underneath it. See?"

Granddad Patterson said he saw, and he liked the idea.

"What's your second sermon going to be about?"

The youngster's patience was tried.

"I told you, Granddad. Once you know about the umbrella, that's all you need to know."

Patterson said, "But what are you going to tell the folks who come to church the next week?"

Jamie said, "I'm going to say let's all go outside and play baseball."

Lenten Sacrifices

It was the first Sunday of Lent, and the sanctuary at Trinity United Methodist Church in Little Rock was appointed for the occasion.

Right after the offering was taken, the Rev. William D. Elliott had the children down front for their sermonette.

"What do we see here today that's different?" Mr. Elliott asked the children.

One said, "The cross"—a special cross was there, made from a tree.

Yes, the cross.

"What else?"

A child said, "The crown of thorns."

Yes, most certainly. The crown of thorns was special there this day.

Mr. Elliott asked, "And do we see anything else different?"

A child said, "All that money in the plates."

Cindy Potter, age six, came home from Sunday school in Pine Bluff reporting mass confusion among her classmates.

The question was, "What will I give up for Lent?"

A boy across the row from Cindy was at a loss.

"All I've got to give up is toys," this boy said, "and God already has all the toys He wants."

It was the same for everybody else.

A boy named David said, "I could give up watching cartoons, but cartoons are so dumb, God probably wouldn't like half of them."

In the end, only Cindy Potter and her friend Amanda knew what to give up.

"We gave up trying to figure out what it means."

Donald Raney of Harrison recalls the sacrifice made by young Drew Pickard.

"The Air Force family of Lt. Col. Joe Pickard were discussing the Lenten season and each member began telling what he or she planned to give up."

The Pickards are on duty on Iceland now, but they'll be coming home to Arkansas.

Drew Pickard was four years old.

When his turn came to declare, Drew hesitated.

Then he said, "I'm going to give up mouthwash."

When Lent was discussed, and the matter of sacrifice, Nicole Goodwin of Little Rock searched her heart.

She would give up McDonald's cheeseburger.

"You have to know Nicole," says Jim Goodwin of his twelve-year-old. "She loves McDonald's cheeseburgers just about better than anything."

So it was not a frivolous bargain.

Saturday, a friend visited, and time came to think about lunch.

The girls decided they would be driven to McDonald's.

Jim Goodwin issued a gentle reminder.

"You know what your agreement is. About Lent?"

His daughter thought about it.

She said finally, "Wendy's will be all right."

Getting Past Those Layers Of Clothes

In their El Dorado Sunday school class, Joyce Finley asked her children, mostly five-year-olds, what made spring so wonderful.

They went around the room.

"Sunshine," a child said.

Joyce Finley liked that.

"Beautiful flowers," offered the second.

The teacher enthusiastically approved.

"Easter," said the third.

Ah, yes, Easter.

The roll call ended abruptly on No. 4 when a girl named Tricia said with a sigh, "It's because your mother doesn't get so worn out putting on all your dammit-hold-still clothes."

Clean, Methodized, Headed North

At Conway, four-year-old Blair Hendrickson got home from church school study hour.

It was noon, and Blair's mother told him to wash up for lunch.

The youngster went into the bathroom and came right out again, confused.

"Mother, Miss Barbara told us we're supposed to wash up only the Lord. What am I supposed to do about my hands and clothes?"

Blair Hendrickson might get with Tammy Homard for a discussion.

She came in and announced to her mother that she had been methodized.

"Methodized?"

Yes, Tammy said, so had her father, her Aunt Dorothy—the whole lot of them, all methodized.

Mrs. H.T. Homard got the youngster slowed down long enough to learn that a small friend from school had just been baptized.

That friend was a Baptist.

It was clear enough to Tammy what had happened to all the Methodist Homards.

Just as it was clear to Charles Sheldon how to lead the lost to God.

On the second night of the big revival, the grownups couldn't get five-year-old Charles ready for church.

He kept looking for something.

"What in the world do you need?" somebody asked.

Charles said he had to find his dad's new hunting compass.

"For church? Why do you need a compass for church?"

Charles said, "Because there's lost folks down there. I heard that preacher say so."

Some Previously Unknown Words Of Christ

Scott Cummings, age four, lives in Prairie Grove.

The youngster received a New Testament, and he was reading the account of the crucifixion to his little brother, Eric, age two.

Reading is not the precise word. But Michael and Mary Cummings, parents of the two boys, listened with pride and then amazement as Scott recalled his church school lesson enough to provide the words:

"Jesus was nailed to the cross along with two other men who were real criminals. Jesus looked down at the people gathered there and said, 'Hey, I didn't do it. These two other guys did.'"

From the Trinity Cathedral Parish weekly publication *The Message:*

"Katie Menees, age two-and-a-half, daughter of Marian and Martin, puts to good use what she learns in Children's Chapel. At the grocery store, Katie found herself restricted to a shopping cart and she wanted down."

She announced in a loud, clear voice, "And now for a parable about Jesus. And Jesus said, I HAVE TO GET OUT OF THE SHOPPING CART RIGHT NOW!"

The Message asks, "Now let's see, was that in the Sermon on the Mount or perhaps the story of the Prodigal Son?"

Babes In The Woods Get Taken For A Ride

From all directions they came back to Hester's Chapel Church of Christ.

Hester's Chapel is five miles west of Paron, in the Ouachita Mountains near Lake Winona.

Five miles as the crow flies.

The old wagons took routes less direct.

At the reunion, if you got still and listened, you could hear the old wagons creaking through the woods. Families coming to church.

Smokey Turbyfill was at the Hester's Chapel reunion.

"Potluck dinner on the ground. Everybody getting together. The best way to wind up a vigorous and inspiring Sunday morning service."

Later, one by one, the families said goodbye.

But, of course, this time they did not leave in wagons. They left in cars and trucks.

A few stayed behind. To visit and to remember old times.

Especially that one day.

Anybody who ever went to Hester's Chapel Church of Christ knew which day that was.

Smokey Turbyfill listened to the old-timers.

"The culprit of that day will remain nameless for his own sake, even though now it is fifty years later."

The worship procedures never varied.

"All the wagons were pulled up fairly close to each other. And it was the custom to leave sleeping infants and toddlers in the shaded wagon beds."

In hot times, children on pallets. In cold, children wrapped in blankets.

Sleeping the sleep of innocent babes.

The only witnesses to the crime were the horses and the mules.

"They were busy with their own feed bags, too busy to care what the young culprit was doing. He was moving here and there among the wagons, switching innocent babes from one wagon to another."

The motive?

"I couldn't find out what prompted the culprit," says Smokey Turbyfill. "But I do know he even swapped his own baby brother."

Those old roads were long and winding.

"Most of the folks had reached their homes and turned their horses and mules loose in the pastures before they noticed they had the wrong child."

It was chaos.

"Mothers were screaming. Older children were laughing their heads off. Fathers were out there in the pasture, hollering un-Christian things, chasing their teams. Did you ever try to catch a mule after he was released late in the evening?"

At nightfall, you could hear wagons charging up and down the roads in all directions.

One old-timer heard a man shout, as a wagon thundered by his house, "I don't know who it is. But with that red hair, it's bound to be a Drennan or a Curtis."

Years later, the way things turned out, some families were never convinced they got the right youngun back.

In the Presence of the Lord?

Tractor Church

As we passed through Bismarck, four men were holding tractor church out in somebody's front yard.

Tractor church occurs between the hours of 11 a.m. and noon on Sunday. Participants gather where somebody has a new tractor. (A truck will do.) The vehicle is discussed, along with other important matters.

As we passed through, one participant was leaving the meeting, which was all right because another was driving up. You need four to avoid the appearance of backsliding.

Tractor church breaks up when the other churches let out, freeing wives and mothers to go home and put dinner on the table.

Can I Get An Amen From The Corner?

To celebrate the 107th anniversary of its founding, Pilgrim's Rest Baptist Church up in Baxter County this Sunday will have an old time religion day.

Pilgrim's Rest Church is on the Monkey Run Road, about one mile west of state Highway 126.

For exact directions, you could ask anybody at Gassville.

Folks at Cotter can tell you where Gassville is.

We know where all these places are, having been fortunate enough as a youngster to spend summers visiting grandparents in the much larger town of Mountain Home, population then well above two thousand. Even so, we did not look down on anybody.

Unless it was on Missouri. Missouri was, and still is, a few miles to the north, with its stateline liquor stores. When you looked up at Missouri, you had enough to look down on.

This coming Sunday at Pilgrim's Rest Church, on the 107th anniversary, the Rev. Estel T. Grigg will preach on "Why I Believe in Old Time Religion."

Up at stateline, people will be lucky who are not working that day.

But the preaching will be only part of it.

To re-create how things were back in 1872, the year the church was founded, Pilgrim's Rest members will dress in old-timey clothes. Several already have said they plan to walk to church and await the arrival of their pastor.

The Rev. Estel Grigg will arrive on horseback.

To go with Mr. Grigg's sermon, there will be a Hallelujah Offering, an Amen Corner, and a close-out with The Lord's Supper.

New timers might not know what an Amen Corner is.

The old church was a long, straight room with a platform up front. The platform did not extend to the walls, but left space open on both sides of the preacher.

In these corners sat deacons or stewards or elders, strong men of the church, to amen important things said by the preacher. The amens heated up with the sermon.

"So the Lord sent the flood."

"Amen."

"Next time He'll send the fire."

"Amen!"

"I forgot to say something in the announcements about tomorrow night's taffy-pulling."

"A-MEN!"

"And next Saturday's sack race in the field next to the church."

"YES-AMEN!!!"

You don't hear this much any more. Most of the lay leadership has been dispersed around through the congregation. The amening doesn't frighten the preacher as much, but still represents a threat to the young people.

Blessed Sleep—
The Enlightened,
Modern-Day View

John Paul Hess of North Little Rock asked his mother why they built Sunday school so close to church.

Mrs. Paul Hess didn't quite understand.

So John Paul, recently turned six, explained: "The whole time I was in nursery and we were supposed to take naps on the pallets, nobody could sleep because everybody was singing and preaching through the walls."

Mrs. Hess asked where John Paul would put the nursery.

The child said, "I'd put it right in there with church. Then the little children could sleep like Uncle Eugene, and you wouldn't even have to have pallets."

The earlier church would not have put up with Uncle Eugene.

Somebody in charge of Christian alertness would have come down the aisle carrying a long stick with a feather on the end of it. This person would have pointed the stick in the pew and tickled Uncle Eugene on the nose with the feather.

Nowadays slumber is recognized as beneficial to Sunday morning procedures. Or if not recognized, then at least it is officially engaged in.

A woman who teaches a Sunday school class, of which her pastor is a member, told us they had to wake him up recently so he could go in and preach.

"He gave a good sermon," she said.

We have here the current *Boone County Historian*. It contains material by Dorothy Sharp, who wrote a history of the First Christian Church of Harrison.

The time was around the turn of the century.

"The minutes reveal," she notes, "that discipline within the church was strict. Any member acting in a manner unbecoming a Christian would find himself playing host to a committee from the church."

It was not a fun-filled occasion.

"He would be asked to stop his actions. If he failed to do so, a second call was made. He was then asked to stop and to appear before members at Wednesday evening services and apologize for embarrassing them. If he refused and other calls brought no results, he was notified that the church would withdraw from him."

In other words, the unbecoming Christian threw himself out.

We talked with a minister friend about Uncle Eugene's recurring Sunday morning naps, even without a pallet.

Would this minister send a committee around with the alternatives—either wake up, Uncle Eugene, or throw yourself out?

By no means would the minister do that.

He explained, "Some people comprehend the Lord's word with much greater clarity when they are not entirely conscious. They might not know as much, but what they know is generally correct."

Of greater concern to our minister friend were those of his flock who knew everything about the Lord wide awake, and most of it was wrong.

"I'd probably put Uncle Eugene in charge of the long pole with the feather on it. But only if it didn't interfere with his worship."

We know a man, a religious fellow, although no bishop, who tells time in church on Sunday by the sound of a loud clunk on the wall behind him.

This fellow sings in the choir, sitting in the back row.

The intensity of his involvement in the services is an inspiration to all.

It begins with a narrowing of the choir member's eyes soon after the preliminaries are over and the minister begins his morning message—"I am talking from the first chapter of..."—a narrowing of the eyes followed shortly by a thoughtful listing of the head.

Within minutes, this good man is also taking the message in through his mouth, his jaws having been unhinged slightly. Presently he is so engrossed, a visitor might mistake it for a coma.

The clunk on the wall is the sound of his own head snapping back, striking it. It is his cue to stand and sing the closing hymn. If the clunk precedes the choir a bit, no matter. He needs a moment to find his songbook.

Make a Joyful Noise, No Matter What

When that soprano lost her skirt on the way to the choir loft at First Baptist Church in Batesville, only her fellow choir members know what happened next.

The soprano loosened her waistband to combat the heat she would encounter in the loft.

The first thing she knew, her skirt was down around her ankles.

Ideally, she would have fainted.

But that did not happen. We know that the choir continued its procession.

Whether the soprano kicked her skirt free, or reached down and jerked it up—the answer is locked behind the smiles of her fellow choir members.

Of course, even some of the choir doesn't know what happened.

Another soprano hissed at the male singers, "If you look, you'll go blind!"

Norman Haley lives in Mabelvale.

"I have been active in church choir music for almost thirty years, most of it here at Life Line Baptist Church in southwest Little Rock."

He recalls that special music program. It was either for Christmas or Easter.

"The idea was that the choir would march down the outside aisles of the sanctuary and into the choir loft while singing."

The choir director put strong emphasis on memorizing the music.

"This was so we could watch him, and also look where we were going, while singing."

One choir member did not memorize the music.

It was something he would never forget again.

The sanctuary's outside aisles had heating grates.

"Coming down the aisle, single file, one of the ladies got her high heel shoe stuck in a grate."

She was cool.

"Rather than create a distraction from the reverence of the moment, the choir member stepped out of her shoe and kept going, not missing a step or a note."

Behind her was another cool one.

"The next person behind her saw what happened. He reached down without breaking stride and gave the shoe a quick jerk."

The shoe came up. But so did the grate, leaving a hole in the floor.

What we had then, to reconstruct the reverent scene, is one choir member coming along, bobbing from side to side like Walter Brennan, and behind her another choir member singing away, his arms full of sheet music and a grating and a woman's shoe.

Behind those two came the singer who had not memorized his music.

"This fellow was having to *look* at his music. He did not see what went on in front of him."

He stepped into the hole in the aisle.

With any mercy at all, he would have put both feet in and dropped immediately to his reward.

But no.

Norman Haley will go no further with his account.

He says simply that in the blink of an eye, the special moment went from reverent to tumultuous.

Mrs. Bob Rosenwinkle of McRae declares that there is more to singing in a church choir than having your skirt drop off or falling through a hole in the floor.

Mrs. Rosenwinkle reports on a choir practice in a small church near Searcy:

"One lady opened her mouth a little too wide. A fly flew into her mouth."

The choir member went into a frenzy of coughing and spitting.

"The other choir members though she was having an attack of some sort."

They wrestled the woman to submission, commanding her to calm down and hush her mouth.

"They finally let her open her mouth long enough to spit out the fly. That showed everybody what the problem was."

When order was restored, the choir resumed rehearsing.

"The next song to be practiced was 'I'll Fly Away.'"

Then there was an episode at First Methodist Church in Magnolia.

A new choir director was met by singers with great enthusiasm.

One said, "We are really looking forward to your helping us with our problem areas. Especially with birth control."

She meant to say breath control.

The choir member turned and walked stiffly away, not even trying to explain.

Visit Again, Tall Stranger, and Thanks For The Bread

If Marie Kennedy had it to do over, she certainly would not hit the stranger right there in church.

Would not hit him with a loaf of bread.

Or tell him where to go.

All the poor man was doing was visiting for a Sunday.

The important thing, Marie Kennedy wants the tall stranger in the corduroy jacket to know, is that other members at Southwest Christian Church in Little Rock are not as aggressive as she is.

Everybody would like for the stranger to visit again.

To understand what happened, you have to hear the explanation offered by Marie Babrick Kennedy herself.

"I baked several loaves of bread on Saturday and decided to take two of them to friends in my church."

This is Marie Kennedy, filling in the background that will explain her behavior.

"On Sunday morning I put the bread in a sack and my husband and I drove to church."

The loaves were for Marie's friends, Bonnie Barnes and Alaska Houston.

"Before the services, I did not have the opportunity to give either friend the bread. I thought I could easily give them the package directly after church."

But did things work out that way?

Things did not.

When church turned out, Mrs. Kennedy needed a lasso.

"Both friends immediately went out different doors and headed toward their cars, which were parked in opposite directions."

The bread delivery was going to require teamwork.

"I realized if I were to give the bread to my friends, Bonnie and Alaska, my husband and I would have to also go different directions."

Marie Kennedy assumed that her husband was directly behind her.

She dug into the sack of homemade bread.

They would have to act quickly.

Mrs. Kennedy pulled out one of the loaves.

Without looking, she passed the bread, whapping her husband smartly on the arm for emphasis "Here, take this to Alaska."

That should have done it.

"When he did not take the bread, I looked up. Instead of seeing my tall husband in a gold corduroy jacket, I saw a tall stranger with a gold corduroy jacket."

The stranger's mouth was open, but nothing came out.

"My husband had ducked into the restroom. The stranger with the same coat had just happened to move up by my side."

It wasn't merely that Marie Babrick Kennedy struck the visitor with a loaf of bread.

Her instructions were even worse.

"He was a stranger who knew nothing about Alaska being in Little Rock."

Alaska, in this case, used to be Alaska Clary.

She acknowledges that being Alaska Houston can be almost fulltime work.

It's sort of like being named Minnesota Pittsburgh.

"Somebody is always saying something."

Alaska Houston got her loaf of bread. She hopes the tall stranger will visit again.

Bountiful Bar-Coded Harvest

Our girl Ruth Marlin went back home to Red Lion, Pennsylvania, to visit her mother.

Her arrival coincided with Harvest Home.

"Harvest Home is a tradition that goes back as far as anybody can remember. In the fall of the year, everybody brings something from home. Something you grew, or something you cooked or preserved. That sort of thing."

The harvest is brought to the church, where it becomes an ever-growing display.

"They put all these goods up on some bleachers inside the church near the altar. Everybody can see who's bringing what. The biggest pumpkin. The longest gourd. The fattest whatever."

And when all the harvest is home, it is turned over to the preacher and his family.

Ruth Marlin is good about going back to Red Lion. But it has been many years since she arrived there at Harvest Home time.

Frankly, Ruth was shocked.

"Years ago the inside of the church looked like a rural painting. Down here on one side were all these cornstalks. Stalks at the other side, too. Everything seemed to be framed in cornstalks."

In between were the pumpkins and the gourds and the preserves and relishes—the bountiful harvest itself.

"I remember bushels of beautiful potatoes."

Scenes of her girlhood. As though it were yesterday.

"The first thing I saw this year when I got to Harvest Home was macaroni."

Somebody had gone to the grocery store and harvested a big bag of it. Elbow macaroni.

"Right next to the macaroni was some brownie mix. Or maybe that was the instant potatoes. Do you hear what I am saying?"

Ruth Marlin, herself, did not seem to hear what she was saying. It is an immense distance from Mom's apple pie, steaming in the bleachers, to a box of instant brownie mix.

"Where the pumpkins used to be, I believe that's where the microwave products were displayed."

Let us come rejoicing, fetching in the pepperoni pizzas. With extra cheese.

Traitorous Tongues

B.R. Collier, a retired minster who lives near Hot Springs, has a collection of cardboard fans appropriated from the churches he served as a visiting preacher.

Each of the fans evokes a memory, but none more than one acquired from a small church in Montgomery County. Mr. Collier would forget it, but his family won't let him.

Sarah Collier recalls her husband's work that morning.

"It was one of those terribly hot days before air conditioning when breathing itself wan't easy and nobody thought twice about fanning right on through the prayer. The little church was packed."

Down on one knee, weaving somewhat, his suit soaked through, Mr. Collier toiled on with the prayer, recounting how much everybody had to be thankful for. A large drop of perspiration clung to his nose.

Mrs. Collier can describe this because she peeped. She saw her husband reach around to his back pocket for a handkerchief, which came free only with a jerk and at the same time fell from his hand.

"He had to open his eyes, and in that split second he saw what was going on in the congregation."

What he saw went to Mr. Collier's head. His next utterance, in one of those moments in which the tongue is seized by unspeakable foolishness and goes off on it own, was to pray:

"Lord, be with our friends who are in their sickbeds and give special comfort to their families and their fans."

The tongue can be a traitorous thing.

We know a woman who moved back to her parents' home with three small children after the untimely passing of her husband.

The young widow's father was a minister, which magnified the difficulties of readjustment.

For one thing, in married life she had taken up smoking. Naturally, she stopped the habit and never mentioned it under her father's roof.

Or she didn't mean to mention it.

At supper one evening, one of the children was pouting about some vegetables. Her mother, nervous and preoccupied with her own problem, blurted impatiently, "Why, Janie, you *know* you like cigarettes!"

She meant to say squash.

A Craighead County minister, who shall be nameless, was leading his Bible study group.

He recited these words from Jesus, "I was thirsty and ye gave Me drink.

"I was hungry and ye gave Me food."

What the minister said next just sort of happened on its own.

He meant to say, "I was in prison and ye visited Me, I was naked and ye clothed Me."

But what came out was, "I was naked and ye visited Me."

Our person on the scene reports that the lesson never quite got back on track.

We know a fellow, the son of a minister, whose family served Sunday dinner to a visiting church official of large importance.

The church official also had a large nose.

Children were cautioned ahead of time not to stare— this was really some nose—and certainly not to say anything about it during the meal.

All went smoothly until the after-dinner coffee was brought around.

That's when one of the children, being helpful, passed the bowl and spoon and said politely, "Dr. Brown, would you care for some sugar in your nose?"

Falling Down For The Lord

Carolyn Crane of Fort Smith emphasizes that there is nothing funny about this, but when her husband, Don, stood up in church for the final hymn Sunday, his left foot, having gone to sleep, buckled under him and he pitched sideways into the aisle.

Help came immediately.

"We have good people in our church. Two men assisted Don quickly back into the pew on his one good foot."

Mrs. Crane says that a third man tried to help. The third man was of no assistance because he was laughing so hard, although certainly there was nothing to be laughed at.

"My husband stood through the hymn like a stork, and I have never heard so many versions of that song mouthed by so many worshipful people trying to get their minds on their business."

At hymn's end things were just about back under control.

Then the associate pastor stood up and dismissed everybody with the benediction "And now unto Him who is able to keep us from falling..."

In His infinite mercy, God saw to it that Crane's two children, ages fourteen and eleven, were at home in bed with severe head colds.

The Nar-What?

This was before the 11 a.m. service at Pulaski Heights United Methodist Church at Little Rock.

A man leaned over and asked his neighbor, "Where would I find the narthex?"

The what?

"The narthex."

The second man sorted through hymnals on the pew rack. "I think it was here just a minute ago. Maybe somebody at the early service..."

But the inquirer said no.

"N-a-r-t-h-e-x. It relates to a person's hearing."

The second man said, oh, *that* narthex.

"It's right behind the Eustachian tube."

Explaining the location, the second man in the pew enunciated broadly so his neighbor with the problem could see the words: "bee-hind-the-you-stay-shun-choob."

To which the questioner replied, with the same large, well-rounded words, "I-can-hear-all-right-but-what-does-this-mean?"

Her referred to a notice on the back page of the church bulletin: "Hearing enhancement devices are available in the narthex."

Oh, *that* narthex.

That particular narthex, according to the dictionary, is "an enclosed passage between the main centrance and the nave of a church."

The *nave?*

"NAVE. The principal longitudinal area of a church, extending from the main entrance or narthex to the chancel, usually flanked by aisles of less height and breadth. Generally only used by the congregation."

In other words, we are talking about the lobby of the church, the narthex, and where the people go in and sit down, the nave.

We asked our acquaintance Reid about the narthex and the nave.

Reid prides himself on a superior knowledge of religious matters.

"Most people are so ignorant of the church," Reid said, "they ought to have to buy tickets to get in."

So where were the narthex and the nave?

Reid replied, "They are right there where they belong. With the apse."

The apse?

"Absolutely. These are all trick words, used to make up crossword puzzles."

Confronted with dictionary facts, Reid dismissed the whole business as architect talk.

"Architects will say anything—'Let us access the nave from the narthex'—and the first thing you know, everybody is going around acting like it makes sense."

Congregation Really Fired Up Over Sermon

At Trinity United Methodist Church Sunday morning they consecrated the new sanctuary.

Bishop Richard B. Wilke came to the church on Little Rock's Mississippi Avenue and preached the sermon.

His title was "The Church Aflame."

Brother, he got that right.

Mere hours before Bishop Wilke stood to deliver "The Church Aflame," eight fire trucks roared up to Trinity and firemen battled a blaze at an education building.

We have heard from half the congregation.

"Do you want to hear a hot one?" a member of the board asked.

"I'll tell you what," said another. "When people got to church and saw the sermon topic in the bulletin, they were practically rolling in the aisles."

This is from a newspaper account of the Saturday afternoon fire at Trinity Church: "Rev. F. Gladwin Connell, senior pastor of the church, estimated the damage at between $250,000 and $300,000. However, the Fire Department put the damage at $75,000."

We discussed this large difference in estimates with the pastor.

Mr. Connell said, "When I made my estimate, the building was still on fire."

The firefighters did an outstanding job, controlling the blaze in twenty minutes.

Oh, yes. The organ prelude that led to Bishop Wilke's "Church Aflame" sermon was "Bring a Torch, Jeanette Isabella."

A Rain of Fiery Coals on All Saints

Estimates of how many fiery coals rained down on the head of the Rev. Truman Welch as he twirled the thurible Sunday morning, those estimates, according to Father Welch himself, are exaggerated.

Father Welch was twirling the thurible at St. Mark's Episcopal Church in Little Rock.

Before a packed congregation, he was censing the altar.

Then, at the top of its arc, the thurible paused like the loop-the-loop ride on a carnival midway, gathering strength for the downward plunge. That's when the thurible's lid came loose.

And fiery coals rained down.

Our correspondent was packed in there with the rest of the folks.

For the Festival of All Saints.

"St. Mark's was packed to the rafters with friends and relatives of maybe four hundred babies waiting to be baptized.

"St. Mark's was packed to the rafters with Hog fan Episcopalians there to express their heartfelt thanks for the excellent season, and an opportunity to have a theme party on New Year's.

"St. Mark's was packed to the rafters with parishioners there to observe the Festival of All Saints.

"St. Mark's was packed to the rafters with parishioners who had already turned in their pledge cards and who, therefore, were not afraid of being cornered by zealous members of the Stewardship Committee.

"It was a fine Sunday to be at St. Mark's."

Our correspondent reports that the St. Mark's choir, attired in red cassocks, formed a line that stretched back about one mile.

"The thurifer, Father Welch, was swinging smoke with such abandon that the choir had every appearance of being a red and white freight train coming down the aisle.

"Things settled into the Episcopalian way of doing church—you know, when you figure out what book you're supposed to have open, you look around and realize you're the last one standing."

All those babies got baptized, with plenty of squalling.

Our correspondent closes in on the fiery scene.

"At the offertory, as the choir rared back and sang praises to famous men, Father Truman Welch, decked out in the finest festival brocaded vestments, decided that just a touch more incense was all we needed to really make this festival day special.

"He started swinging the thurible with abandon. Round and round it went, smoke billowed, worshipers leaned forward in their pews to get a better view of this bronco priest twirling a thurible like a lasso."

Right then was when it happened.

"Father Welch lost his momentum in mid-swing. The thurible swung up, hung for a second upside-down, and then the top came clattering off, and burning coals were heaped down on needlepointed cushions. Father Welch's head would have been better!"

Those sharp intakes of breath came from members of St. Cecelia's Needlework Guild, realizing their work was on fire.

Now on the double came St. Mark's rector, the Rev. Ted Glusman. "Fr. Glusman wrestled with Fr. Welch for the privilege of being seen rushing the burning cushion from the church. Out the back door the two priests went, in solemn procession, bearing the smoldering cushion."

And that was that.

We have visited with Father Welch, who acknowledged that he did swing the thurible with exuberance.

Contrary to reports, however, his hair did not catch fire.

"One of my hands. It got burned in a couple of places."

The Song Is More Beautiful Than That

Our friend Reid is worried because his mind wanders in church.

It comes with no warning.

The preacher can be up there reading from Philippians.

Or giving an important announcement.

Or blessing the collection plates.

Reid's mind gets up and eases out of the pew. Turns up the aisle. Heads out the door. His mind disappears down the street, with no more Christian sense of direction than a dried-up oak leaf lurching through an October neighborhood.

Worried is not quite the word for it.

Reid knows he can't sneak this thing past the Lord any more than you can sneak sunrise past a rooster.

Reid told us that if a wandering mind is a sin, he just hopes to hell it's not one of the Big Ones.

Reid's mind has been wandering in church (wandering out of church) since his feet stuck straight out in the pew.

Back when he thought Philippians were Philippinos. "Good work!"

Those words were written on a piece of paper by the giant of a man who sat beside young Reid every Sunday morning.

The words judged some crayon work in Reid's lap.

Do you think it was the Lord's business? The Baby Jesus? Some lambs?

The crayon work was, in fact, a black haystack with a red faucet angling out at the top.

Young Reid's version of a Thanksgiving turkey.

Years later, many years, he found that work on the day the family buried the giant. He turned out to be five feet, nine inches.

Reid's mind wandered wildly through the funeral service.

He was running to catch up with his father. One last time. To say to him, "Good work!"

In his worst moments, Reid fears detection.

He gets the idea that everybody in church can read his vagrant thoughts.

Reid becomes so convinced of this, he stands invisible in the aisle and looks into the pew at himself, fingers laced between his knees, mouth slightly open.

This division lasts only a second before Reid is reunited with himself, swallowing a dry swallow, looking around to determine whether anybody else saw his mind return.

"A good preacher has the hardest job in the world," Reid said. "Do you want me to tell you why?"

We were drifting in the middle of Lake Ouachita. The alternative to hearing was to go over the side.

"I am *aware* of God!" Reid's statement cracked the air, cracked it and then rolled out across the lake's surface in all directions.

We considered going over into ninety feet of water.

"A preacher's problem," Reid said, "is he has to spend ninety percent of his pulpit time trying to raise the congregation's awareness level."

Reid said he was already aware of God—not booming it this time, not scaring the fish—and moreover, God was aware of his awareness.

"But the preacher, bless his heart, he has to keep coming after it, keep coming every Sunday, until if you're already aware of God, it begins to sound like the marching band at halftime when all the musicians turn away from the field microphone except for the trombones. I mean, it's strong, but the song is more beautiful than that."

It made Reid's mind wander.

"Sometimes I have the urge to go up there and get the preacher by the elbow and whisper to him, 'Let's get out of here.'"

We asked Reid why he was telling us all of this.

Our friend had put his casting rod down. His hands were laced between his knees, his mouth slightly open.

"Telling you all what?" he said.

He is a man in trouble.

And not getting any younger.

CHARLES ALLBRIGHT has been a reporter, editorial writer, and columnist for the *Arkansas Gazette* since 1955, except for seven years spent as a speech writer for Governor Winthrop Rockefeller. He has written the *Arkansas Gazette*'s "Arkansas Traveller" column since 1974.